The Compassionate Leader

The Compassionate Leader offers an honest and refreshing guide to leading schools with purpose and heart. Drawing from the author's personal experiences as a school leader, interviews with head teachers and the latest research, this inspiring book demonstrates that compassionate leadership is not a soft alternative to strong leadership – but the cornerstone of strong leadership itself.

This book explores the key skills of 'compassionate leadership' and how they can be used in a school context to get the best out of yourself, your staff and your pupils. Covering values and ethos, coaching and professional development, well-being strategies and much more, the chapters reveal how you can create cultures of trust, inclusion and psychological safety, where everyone from support staff to families feel seen, heard and valued.

Packed with actionable strategies and reflective insights, this is essential reading for all current and aspiring school leaders wanting to create a healthy and authentic culture where the whole school community can thrive.

Sarah Hussey is a former head teacher who began her career as a midday supervisor and now brings her 25 years of educational and leadership experience to her work as a performance coach, keynote speaker, trainer and author.

'This book is brilliant; deeply honest, full of fascinating research and most importantly practical ideas to support school leaders navigating the stormy seas of working in Education. Sarah openly shares her leadership story, one which is dangerously close to that of so many fantastic school leaders and indeed my own.

It hits hard with vital messages for leaders currently serving in schools, and those who may have left their roles, about how to develop awareness of physical and emotional health and signs of burnout. She pairs the stark data with real examples calling out practises which are damaging to the health and wellbeing of educators across the country.

Sarah's exploration of what it means to align values, to belong, and to lead with compassion and kindness are refreshing and powerful. If you have left leadership read this to know you are not alone, and if you are still serving in Educational Leadership read it to better understand how you can protect yourself and your teams from some of the storms that threaten to engulf you.'

Emma Lewry, Early Education Consultant
and Former Headteacher, UK

'I guess it depends if you are content with just forcing compliance or whether you have the appetite to strive for commitment? Your call?

If your staff are compliant to your wishes then you will never get there. If your pupils are compliant to your teaching, it will be hard work and their growth will be compromised!

But if you can gain the commitment from staff and pupils, then with commitment comes engagement, dialogue, ownership, innovation, well-being, happiness and performance. Now I reckon that is worth working toward and that is where compassion comes in. Sarah Hussey shines a clear and bright light on the power that a compassionate leader wields. In this excellent and most readable exposé, Sarah makes a compelling argument that leading with kindness, courage and purpose is precisely what's needed in our education system. These are super-powers, not weaknesses. Anyone can shout and demand, and they will get what they deserve. But to lead in such a way that through nurturing your understanding of others and then responding with positive intent you gain their commitment, their energy and their effort, is a no-brainer to me.

Now, I have taken on many challenges in my life, but I have never spent a wet Friday afternoon in a reception class with no teaching assistant! How would I manage I wonder? I know the outcome I would like (an enthusiastic sea of smiling, attentive faces hanging on my every word), and I believe that Sarah knows how to get there and how to help others do the same. Read on and you will too!'

Manley Hopkinson, Director of the Compassionate
Leadership Academy, UK

'Reading Sarah's book feels like sitting with a trusted friend and putting the world to rights. It makes you feel seen and heard and reminds you you're not alone. It is a distillation of her wisdom, wit and warmth and chock-full of practical tips and rich research for exactly the kind of authentic and compassionate leadership our schools so desperately need today. For so long now, school leadership has felt for many an impossible step too far, requiring the sacrifice of any life outside school and the compromise of values – but if you follow Sarah's guidance, you CAN make it work.'

Dr. Emma Kell, Teacher and Education Coach, UK

The Compassionate Leader

Shaping Schools with Kindness, Courage and Purpose

Sarah Hussey

LONDON AND NEW YORK

Designed cover image: © Getty Images

First published 2026
by Routledge
4 Park Square, Milton Park, Abingdon, Oxon OX14 4RN

and by Routledge
605 Third Avenue, New York, NY 10158

Routledge is an imprint of the Taylor & Francis Group, an informa business

© 2026 Sarah Hussey

The right of Sarah Hussey to be identified as author of this work has been asserted in accordance with sections 77 and 78 of the Copyright, Designs and Patents Act 1988.

All rights reserved. No part of this book may be reprinted or reproduced or utilised in any form or by any electronic, mechanical, or other means, now known or hereafter invented, including photocopying and recording, or in any information storage or retrieval system, without permission in writing from the publishers.

For Product Safety Concerns and Information please contact our EU representative GPSR@taylorandfrancis.com. Taylor & Francis Verlag GmbH, Kaufingerstraße 24, 80331 München, Germany.

Trademark notice: Product or corporate names may be trademarks or registered trademarks, and are used only for identification and explanation without intent to infringe.

British Library Cataloguing-in-Publication Data
A catalogue record for this book is available from the British Library

ISBN: 978-1-032-90444-3 (hbk)
ISBN: 978-1-032-90438-2 (pbk)
ISBN: 978-1-003-55808-8 (ebk)

DOI: 10.4324/9781003558088

Typeset in Melior
by codeMantra

To my daughters, Holly and Poppy, who make me a better person with their very existence. Your strength of character and compassion inspire me daily. Life will always be better with you around. I love you.

To my husband, Andrew, who like the Japanese art of Kintsugi put a broken person back together and showed them how beautiful they are. You are the gold that holds us all together. I love you.

Contents

	Preface	x
	Introduction	1
1	What is the research telling us?	2
2	Compassionate leadership and why it matters – be brave, not brutal	14
3	Well-being strategies to avoid burnout and keep your community positive	27
4	Values, ethos and culture – how to grow, sustain and nurture them	49
5	Compassion, coaching and self-efficacy – professional development for the whole team	63
6	Possibilities and perspectives: the future of school leadership	80
	Final thoughts	92
	Index	93

Preface

(Be More Betty)

'The head teacher has successfully developed a school community based on caring and inclusive values'.

In December 2022, I was blue-lighted in an ambulance, across the Solent on a hovercraft to the Queen Alexandra Hospital in Portsmouth. The cardiologist I had seen in my local hospital suspected I had already had two or more heart attacks and that I was building up to a third and more damaging attack. I was wired up to lots of machines, pumped full of drugs and told to stay still and remain relaxed (both of those things are hard for me at the best of times). I was 52 years old with no previous issues with my heart – how on earth did I get here?

In September 2022, I was beginning my 13th year of headship at a primary school on the Isle of Wight. I had worked hard to be there, and I still enjoyed many aspects of the job. There is no doubt that there have been significant changes in the role during that time, some, of course, for the better, but most of them creating more work with less time in which to do it. I was having coaching sessions with a rather wonderful performance coach and educational expert (Dr. Emma Kell), and we were beginning to start to plan beyond headship. However, before we could put together anything concrete, I had the small matter of a very imminent inspection from our 'friends' at Ofsted, which would be my third inspection as head teacher. I imagine if we looked back at those coaching sessions, Emma would say that my thoughts around it were erratic. I had sessions where I was completely confident about how well I knew the school, how great my team was and how we would show them our school community, its values and the collective vision of how to move forward. At other sessions, after hearing from local head teachers about how their recent inspections had gone, I was a gibbering wreck, catastrophising about being graded inadequate due to safeguarding issues that were considered not to be dealt with effectively. Local head teachers of schools like mine who were inspected in the weeks prior to my school described the process as brutal; they felt bullied and undermined and either felt unable to complain or did complain with no satisfactory outcome. I was terrified that the school I loved would be made to join a Multi-Academy Trust and lose all its uniqueness. My imposter syndrome was having a whale of a time, reminding me that I was finally going to be 'outed' as the fraud that I am! The build-up to the inspection really affected me both mentally and physically in a way it had never done before. My blood pressure was already being treated for being too high, but this started to creep up further; I was taking antidepressants and really struggling to sleep. I think that we can all agree that this constant state of stress is never going to end well.

I received 'the call' from Ofsted on the 13th of November, for a section 8 visit on the 14th and 15th November (ironically the same days as Caversham Primary where Ruth Perry was head). The inspection happened as they usually do, and the assessor left saying that we were still 'good', but they would be back within two years to ensure that we hadn't dropped to 'Requires Improvement'. And life went on, just as it had after the previous two … except it did not.

Several days prior to the inspection, I had been told by my general practitioner (GP) to increase the medication I was on for my blood pressure, which I duly did. On day one of the inspection, during our safeguarding grilling, I looked down at my feet and noticed that they were at least twice their normal size! It was reminiscent of Violet Beauregarde in Charlie and the Chocolate Factory when she chewed bubble gum that was not quite ready for consumption! So, I had another chat with my GP and told her my recent blood pressure readings and a photo of my feet. She told me to leave work immediately and rest – I explained that I couldn't possibly as I was in the middle of an inspection. So, I stayed and happily waved the inspector goodbye the next day.

Over the following few weeks, I changed my blood pressure medication and tried to continue to work as normal. Yet, as I said, things didn't just go back to normal – there was no sense of relief or success about our outcome; I did not want to celebrate it in the local press and on social media as I would have done before. I felt that the process had been a real battle and that there was no benefit in it for me as a school leader and certainly none for the staff and children. As a school, nothing had changed. We were still desperately underfunded, understaffed and struggling with the challenging behaviour of some pupils and parents. For the first time as a head teacher, I was really struggling to know how to support my staff and the wider school community. I know many of you will be familiar with this feeling.

At the beginning of December, I went with my year 1 class on a trip to Osborne House, the royal residence of Queen Victoria, to learn about the royal children and what their life would have been like. We all had a wonderful day, and on the bus on the way home a pupil sitting next to me fell asleep on my shoulder. It was at that time that I started to notice that I had pins and needles in my arm and a tight feeling in my chest – I decided I would take my bra off as soon as I got back to school; clearly it was too tight. When we got back to school, I took my blood pressure (extremely high) and emailed the GP. The next morning, I had a phone call from the GP surgery, a nice nurse suggesting that I go up to Accident and Emergency (A&E) for an electrocardiogram (ECG), just to be on the safe side. I remember thinking that it was not possible as I had an assembly with parents to do and some other important things – funny that now I can't remember what those things were. I managed to get to A&E at lunchtime and was told off immediately by the triage nurse for not coming sooner. Once there, I was wired up to an ECG, had some blood tests and was told that they would let me know what was happening. Several hours, ECGs and blood tests later (at 8 pm), I was told that they would be keeping me in and took me up to a ward. Luckily, my kind-hearted friend who had arrived to see what was going on brought with her clean pants, pajamas (PJs) and lots of chocolate – I hadn't eaten all day! At this point, there was no mention of what was wrong, but just that they wanted to be able to keep an eye on my symptoms.

Despite having more chest pain and breathlessness during the night, which the nurses dealt with, I was sent home the next morning. The doctor who discharged me wasn't sure what was wrong with me and suggested I double my medication for acid reflux and gave me a glyceryl trinitrate (GTN) spray to use in case it was angina. I went home and slept like a princess. During the next few days, I didn't really start to feel any better physically but started to convince myself it was anxiety about work and that I could cope. However, I felt so ill by the Wednesday of the following week that I phoned 111 again and was taken back to A&E in an ambulance this time. This time there was no space for me on the ward, but they didn't want to discharge me as my ECG was showing abnormal readings again. And so, I spent the night in A&E – luckily with so much morphine for the pain that I don't remember too much about it. The next morning, I was moved to 'fit to sit' and told that I couldn't go home without seeing a cardiologist. My husband had joined me by then, so we sat, and we waited…and waited. We were quite calm at this point and thought that I would be sent home again. However, when a very efficient consultant joined us, he explained the scenario as he saw it. He did not use the term 'anxiety' in his diagnosis. Firstly, he apologised and said that I should never have been sent home on the previous Saturday morning and went on to explain to me what he thought my ECGs were telling him. His analysis was that I had already had two or three small heart attacks (we later started referring to them as cardiac events) and that all my vital signs were pointing to the fact that I was heading for a bigger and much more serious one, so the best place for me would be the Cardiac Unit in QA Hospital in Portsmouth and that I would be taken there as soon as they could arrange an ambulance and a hovercraft. I was then moved from 'fit to sit' and taken to the cardiac ward where I was wired up to lots of beeping machines, injected with morphine in my arm and blood thinners in my tummy and told once again to stay calm and still. Calm was not how I felt – I was terrified and disappointed with myself for not taking my symptoms seriously. My husband was wonderful, true to form, but he was also terrified – we were suddenly confronted with our own mortality. I cannot tell you how trivial my worries and concerns about school were at this point. I honestly thought that the job I loved was about to kill me.

I ended up spending the night in that ward and then being blue-lighted the next morning to the hovercraft and across to Portsmouth. I remember, both my husband

and father stood watching and waving as they put me in the ambulance – they both looked so worried, and I won't lie it did cross my mind that I wouldn't see them again.

What an adventure it was getting across the Solent, some people in my position get their trip in the air ambulance, but I had a hovercraft all to myself (and the ambulance crew) – who knew the luggage rack would fit a stretcher and beeping machines so well? I couldn't help feeling sorry for all the people waiting for the hovercraft who then weren't allowed on – according to my friend who is now an ambulance driver it happens almost daily. On arrival in Southsea, I was picked up by another amazing paramedic team and taken to QA. I will spare you the details of the next few days, but I had numerous tests, observations and meetings with specialists and was discharged after another three days, with a suitcase full of medicine and a diagnosis of ischemic heart disease, but no one was really sure of the details, but what was clear was the fact it was caused by constantly living in a state of heightened stress.

The overwhelming relief of being home, without having surgery and in time for Christmas, was bloody wonderful – for a couple of weeks! However, I knew hard decisions would have to be made. I left headship in August 2023, too young to take my pension and apparently not unwell enough to qualify for medical retirement.

My story is just one of many.

So, the big question is – how are we, as a profession, going to make the changes that will prevent this in the future and allow education in this country to thrive?

Introduction

I did not set out to write a book about compassionate leadership. I set out to understand why in so many schools, brilliant educators were feeling isolated and overwhelmed, and why, despite their best efforts, school leaders were burning out and leaving the profession. What I discovered along the way was something both simple and profound: compassion isn't just a nice thing to have in education – it is essential.

Compassionate leadership is not a soft alternative to strong leadership – it is strong leadership. It is the courage to listen deeply, the wisdom to act with empathy and the resilience to hold space for others, whilst navigating the pressures of education in our modern world. It is about creating cultures of trust, inclusion and psychological safety – where everyone, students, teachers, support staff and families feel seen, heard and valued.

Whether you are an executive head teacher, a head teacher, a teacher stepping into leadership or someone supporting school communities in different ways, this book is an invitation to reimagine leadership.

It draws on a range of research, from statistics, from science, from the wisdom of inspirational speakers, authors and advisors, and of course from the lived experiences of educators, including myself. The book aims to give practical strategies and reflective insights for those of you who aspire to lead with authenticity, kindness and moral purpose. Each chapter has places where you are invited to 'Take a Moment'. At these intervals you are invited to reflect on your own experiences and plan actionable steps for your future practice.

But more than this, I sincerely hope that it gives you permission to slow down, to listen more deeply and to lead in a way that is true to your values. Leadership isn't about being perfect; it is about being present.

When we lead with compassion, we don't just change schools, we change lives.

What is the research telling us?

This chapter will explore the ideas that

- The school system in England is at breaking point.
- Change is necessary, particularly at leadership level.
- Leaders (positive and negative) have the biggest impact on education at all levels.

What makes a school successful?

Before we begin to unpick the research and identify what it tells us about the current English school system, I want us to visualise the kind of school that would allow pupils, staff and the entire community to thrive and not just survive. What do these schools have? Or maybe the question should be – what do they not have?

Throughout my working life in schools, in numerous roles and different settings, I do not think that any two schools have been exactly the same – however, there are common themes and threads that run through them that make them successful; similarly, there are common themes and threads that hinder their success in significant ways. At this point, does the definition of a 'winning' school need to be examined at all? Or is its success enough of a statement? Many educationalists will have differing opinions about what it means to lead and work in a successful school, what that 'success' looks like and how it is measured.

Below is an imaginary illustration featuring two primary schools, with differing approaches and results. Read how each school operates, identifying their values, successes and challenges, and then decide which school would you prefer to be a part of.

School A

A primary school with a recent good (in all areas) Ofsted rating. According to published data, the year 6 Standard Assessment Tests (SAT) results are above the national average, and children come into school at the age of four with an average baseline assessment. The behaviour policy is clear and concise and is on the school website for everyone to refer to. There is a system of clear sanctions when behaviour is deemed inappropriate, and exclusions have been recorded for children as young as seven. When you visit the school, the corridors are quiet, the pupils look smart in the uniform and in lessons there is an atmosphere of calm and quiet. At breaktimes and lunchtimes, there are no teachers in the staff room, they are working in their rooms, marking and preparing lessons or even supervising pupils that struggle with these less structured times of the day. Teaching staff have staff meetings once a week, morning briefings twice a week and parental drop-ins every fortnight. Each teacher and many support staff run after-school clubs for the pupils. The curriculum seems to focus heavily on reading, writing, maths and science, and there is a set way to teach each lesson and a clear homework policy for each year group. Reports and pupil progress meetings are half-termly. There appears to be a high staff turnover, despite a Wellbeing Policy and Champion in place, although no exit interviews are held with leavers. Staff often do not return after maternity leave as they go and work elsewhere in a part-time role. There is little mention of inclusion or intervention support for pupils on their website.

School B

A primary school with a recent inspection that rated it as good in the areas of Quality of Education, Behaviour and Attendance, and Leadership and Management. The judgement for Personal Development is outstanding. The year 6 SAT results have been in line with the national average for the last three years – previously they were below. Children enter the school at the age of four well below the expected baseline and often with poor speech and language skills. The school's behaviour policy is also available on the school website and is focussed heavily on rewards and restorative conversations, but there are clear sanctions in place. There have been a small number of exclusions for pupils in year 5 and 6 in the last three years. The school has nurture provision and works closely with other professionals. The corridors are not always quiet as many pupils will engage with conversions with the adults that are on duty. Not all pupils are in uniform, there are some pupils without ties and wearing trainers. Classrooms can be quiet when that is expected, but they are also a place where pupils are expected to discuss ideas and share their thoughts and answers. If a visitor arrives, pupils are keen and proud to tell them about their school. Pupils in classrooms are clearly supported by other members of staff, and learning is adapted for them where necessary. Staff meetings have a clear focus on professional learning and do not take place when there are parents' evenings or curriculum sessions for families. Teachers take their Planning, Preparation and Assessment time (PPA) at home and will visit the staff room if they want to during breaks in the school day. This school has a number of teachers who started at the school as volunteers or support staff, and staff turnover is low. There is a Wellbeing Policy but no Champion, and the school has a therapy dog.

During this book, there are moments that have been built in for you to reflect on what you have just read and to think about you would do in certain scenarios. Please take the time to engage with them as they will support you to process your values and your ambitions about your leadership journey.

Take a moment:

- What are your initial thoughts about the two imaginary schools above?

- What do you think the culture of these schools is? How would you find out more?

At first glance, the two schools described above do have certain things in common, including a recent positive report from Ofsted (whether we like it or not they are here to stay!). However, there are some clear differences that suggest that the culture of the schools is not the same – in fact they are probably very different. As the book progresses, we will be able to see this more clearly. I would say that the leaders of these schools have very different skills and core values and that although one school is far more interested in academic success, it is not an inclusive environment, and there are key indicators that staff are not happy or supported well.

School B does not have the same high results, but pupils make good progress, from a lower starting point, supported by a broad and balanced curriculum and an atmosphere of active learning with motivated pupils. Staff would appear to be more settled and valued.

I know which school I would like to work in, send my children/grandchildren to and be proud to lead – but what are the key elements that a 'successful school' needs to encourage?

A school where students and staff will thrive needs a leader with a certain set of skills, who does (not just says) the right things and is not afraid to face up to the 'tough stuff'. When referring to the 'tough stuff', I don't mean sending pupils home because they are wearing the wrong shoes nor following school rules; I mean facing up to why these things might be happening, listening to their communications in whatever form and then finding ways to support pupils and their wider families. These skills are known as soft skills and work well in schools due to the human element of the setting. Importantly, leaders who are compassionate, inclusive and secure in their emotional intelligence will create a set of beliefs that others will buy into and follow. Leaders need to know how to lead, not through fear or expectation of compliance but through building relationships, proving they can be trusted and fostering a sense of belonging. It will be evident why a compassionate leader does what they do, and they will ask you to acknowledge your 'why' and to keep that central to what you do. A leader that inspires you should be someone who is self-aware, thoughtful and open to feedback – in short, someone who cares.

Where do we find these leaders right now? How do we create leaders for the future pupils in our schools? And how do we create more educational settings that are successful for all? I hope this book will go some way towards helping leaders to do this and ultimately change some of the deeply worrying statistics below? After all, I was and am one of those leaders, but I still couldn't prevent myself from burning out.

Heading for crisis – why we need to rethink the way we lead schools

The Teacher Wellbeing Index is an annual report written by Education Support and is based on evidence from surveys with education staff at all levels who were asked a range of questions concerning how they felt in their roles.

The seventh annual report created by them is based on evidence collated during 2023, and the results are more damning than in any other previous year.

Some of the key findings from the Teacher Wellbeing Index 2023 are as follows (based on the results that they had):

78%	School staff are stressed.
82%	Teachers are stressed.
89%	School leaders are stressed.
37%	School leaders are experiencing problems with their mental health.
35%	Of the 35%, say they have symptoms of burnout.
73%	Staff think that Ofsted inspections are not fit for purpose.
73%	Staff think that Ofsted inspections do not improve learner achievement.

This is a tiny snapshot of the evidence produced in the document, which also covers loneliness at work, the high levels of stress experienced, the lack of effective support within the workplace for mental health and worrying statistics about suicidal thoughts and tendencies in school leadership roles.

The impact of stress at work

- In 2021–2022, it is thought that 1694 of all head teachers left their posts earlier than intended, and not due to retirement, in many cases leaving the profession altogether. In the same year, 40,000 teachers left their post, and it is currently thought that 12.8% of ECTs (early career teachers) are leaving after one year (Dr. Becky Taylor: Principal Research Fellow at UCL's Centre for Teachers and Teaching Research).

- A third of all secondary school heads leave the job within a five-year window.
- Recent figures for Initial Teacher Training make worrying reading for the profession, particularly for secondary schools, as only half of the secondary recruitment targets were met for September 2023. These figures are worse than the previous year; when 57% were met, in fact targets were only met in three subjects. If these numbers keep falling, we could be heading for a crisis in teacher recruitment. James Noble-Rogers, Chief Executive of the Universities Council for the Education of Teachers, said the figures made for 'sorry reading'.

They mean that schools, particularly secondary schools, will struggle to recruit the new teachers they need. The government needs, as a matter of urgency, to bring together all relevant stakeholders to agree on a cohesive and fully funded strategy to recruit and retain teachers.

(December 2023)

In February 2023, the Headrest Annual Headteacher Wellbeing Report was also written with very similar and startling findings. This report breaks down the key stressors for head teachers during the year 2021–2022 as the following:

- Moral injury.
- Anxiety, burnout and stress.
- Bullying and intimidation.
- Staff retention.
- Staff recruitment.
- Unintelligent accountability.

The identification of these very specific areas of stress and anxiety for staff should form the basis of trying to improve not only the profession but the educational system as a whole. Some of the indicators may sound all too familiar, but others are newer terms and need to be properly understood if anything is to change.

What does this look like in reality?

Throughout this book, I will examine the factors that indicate strong, yet compassionate leadership and why it is hard to be an effective leader when you feel that you are pressurised to make decisions that are not in the best interests of the communities that you are serving. The report describes this as 'moral injury' and that description resonated with me on a very deep level. The term 'moral injury' is found in caring professions and is identified a lot in the National Health Service (NHS) where professionals are constantly fighting a battle to perform their job in the way they want to but within the restraints of their budgets, which is frequently impossible. This results in constant compromise of their own personal and professional values, which in turn leads to feelings of guilt and shame that build up over time. This is the same for school leaders and teachers as the report states:

> School leaders were often faced with having to make decisions that went against deeply held beliefs and principles due to budget limitations, staffing shortages and/or other constraints. They increasingly found themselves having opt for not the best option but what they deemed as the 'least bad option'.
> (page 9)

Let me give you an example.
Imagine this scenario:
Your year 6 SAT results have been declining over the last two years, and you are under scrutiny from the Local Authority and your School Improvement Partner (SIP) wants to know what your plan of action is. They helpfully give you some suggestions that they have seen work in other schools. Their first suggestion is that you employ a second teacher or a higher-level teaching assistant to work with your cohort of 30 year 6 children, which will enhance their progress. The second suggestion is that you take staff from other year groups to support in year 6. After all some of those classes have one-to-one staff working with individual pupils with identified barriers to learning – so the teacher will not be on their own. The third suggestion is that you focus all the intervention work on the children who might make AREs (age-related expectations) in the tests and give those who won't, a 'project' to be working on independently.

Each of these suggestions comes with their own problems that will cause you as a leader to question what is the morally right thing to do? But remember, you must do something! The first one is in most cases an absolute no as there will not be enough money in the budget to appoint extra members of teaching staff, and if there was, I would question why. The second suggestion would make you think about what is fair for the pupils of the other classes. Is it fair on the pupil who needs that support to be then sharing that resource with the rest of the class? Is it fair or even possible for that member of staff to be a one-to-one and teaching assistant all at once? And thirdly, is it morally right that a particular group of pupils is not experiencing an equitable education as their peers? What would you do? Should we have to stop thinking in terms of what is fair?

I recognise this as something that I struggled with constantly. It got to the point that I almost felt a fraud when advertising the school through open days or social media because as a community we made promises to families about giving them the 'best experiences' and having 'high expectations' when the reality was that sometimes what we could actually provide was nowhere near what I would have described as the best. This plays on your conscience in a way that I think you can only understand if you work in a publicly funded sector with finite resources, where you are responsible for the care and future opportunities of other human beings. It is not a new phenomenon per se but is now more specifically identifiable as a significant source of pressure and stress.

When I secured my headship in 2010, I was 40 years old, but I had only been teaching for 10 years (before that I had 5 years of supporting in classrooms and playgrounds). In so many ways, I was incredibly naive, or perhaps just idealistic – I will leave you to ruminate on that one; I am still undecided.

It was a turbulent time on the Isle of Wight. We were changing from a three-tier school system and moving to a two-tier one. I could write an entire book on the angst that this caused, the drama that unfolded as the plan was played out and the complete lack of direction from anyone to support the schools. There I was a newly qualified head teacher (have I said that I only applied for jobs for interview practice?) of a school who proudly wore its 'outstanding badge' that had been awarded many years previously, sitting right in the centre of a melting pot of local politics and parental outrage. I truly believed that the changes would be in the best interest of the pupils (despite my own mum being a middle school teacher for many years) and so went into my new role with the belief that what I was doing was ethically right. This was a long time before my attention-deficit/hyperactivity disorder (ADHD) diagnosis and before many years of leadership training and coaching; therefore, listening and keeping quiet was still something that I needed to work on. Over the years, when I look back on my first foray into leading, I cringe, thinking of how many people I must have upset with my 'doing it for the greater good' attitude, whilst at other times take pride in the fact that I was so passionate, and so driven to get things right. I think that at those very early meetings, with local councillors and heads whose opinions differed to mine, there were times when you could see my passion lighting up the room – the problem with this is that passion can turn into a fire if you don't control it and end up causing more harm than good.

I remember attending my first local head teacher forum meeting and being utterly horrified at the cynicism, belligerence and downright uncollaborative attitudes of some of the longer standing leaders in the room (this was my perspective – not theirs). I was so sure that what we were embarking on was not only the right thing for the pupils across the Isle of Wight, but equally certain that it would have been already planned like a military operation by those much more supervisory than me, and with more than enough funding to get it right.

Naive, idealistic or just plain stupid?

In many ways, that 'baptism of fire' meant that I developed strategies to think outside the box about how to deliver the best we could and how to use funding creatively. Somewhere at this point I would have done well to discover the 'good enough' theory of Donald Winnicott, which is mentioned later. However, after over a decade of headship, moral injury becomes a very real and frequent occurrence. In the months that led up to my ill health, I was faced with another incident of moral injury that had rumbled for a while, but ended up reaching boiling point, something that I regret. However, my regret is that as a school leader I was put in that position, not regretting the stand that I took. This situation was regarding two very young, very vulnerable pupils that came into our care at the same time. The truth of the situation was that they were both incredibly challenging and found it hard to regulate their emotions, for valid reasons, and so there was a feeling amongst members of the school community that neither child was in the 'right school'. I knew some of the staff who worked with these children were concerned for their own safety (their line manager had kept me updated) as well as that of the other pupils, but I had not realised just how strongly they felt until I had a meeting with them all to see if we could do some problem-solving and look at the situation with a bit of group perspective. During the meeting, some staff were very animated about their views on how they believed children should behave and why they needed to be educated elsewhere; one long-standing member of staff even threatened to leave if I did not do something about the two traumatised children. I am not going to delve too deeply into what followed, suffice to say that the children remained in that class until a change in living arrangements for both meant changes in their education too. The moral part that hurt the most, for me in this situation, was that as a team we had worked hard over many years on building a culture based on compassion – hung on the firm belief that all children deserve the chance of a good education, despite their circumstances. This had been communicated in so many ways over so many years – yet here I was faced with the reality that there were still members of the community that did not stand by this ethos when things got tough. I expected instances of resistance like this at the beginning of my headship, but not 12 years later when I firmly believed we were all working to the same core values.

One of the best pieces of advice I have been given over the years is that just because you have communicated important information doesn't mean that it has always been heard.

Take a moment:

- **As we focus more on the leadership values that we need to be a compassionate leader, it might be a good idea to look back at this real-life scenario and think about what you might have done if faced with the same issue?**

Effective accountability – how much is too much?

I think that the term 'Unintelligent Accountability' is a brilliant description of the accountability measures that schools are judged on – well done to the team at Headrest for coming up with that one. As a head teacher, you soon come to realise that it is not just the visits from Ofsted, but those from your school improvement partners, and the annual safeguarding audits, but also the endless financial and health and safety checks. Of course, you can then add in to the mix the endless statutory testing of the children, a baseline assessment as they enter school, another one at the end of their first year in school, phonics screening (which they pass or fail) in the summer term of year 1, SATs in year 2 (apparently not a requirement anymore, but many schools still do them) and the end of Key Stage 2 (KS2) tests that tell children if they are age related or greater depth. The intensity of these evaluations might make you stop and think about how compassionate we are to the children in our care. As a school leader, I completely recognise and believe in the necessity of accountability and the need to assess our pupils' progress and outcomes, however I would rather see effective formative assessment and adaptive teaching in every lesson, than a barrage of 'tests'. Teachers who use effective strategies daily in their classrooms know their pupils, where their strengths are, their gaps in learning and how they intend to address them; they are the teachers who will improve outcomes for pupils, not the ones with colour-coded spreadsheets.

The importance of supporting roles: we're in this together

There is an interesting section in the Headrest report which categorises the types of problems that head teachers spoke to them about when they called for support, and I am pretty sure that all of us have dealt with at least half of them during our time leading schools. They are:

- **Occasional rogue governors.**
- **Problematic parents.**
- **Lack of specialist support for students with Special Educational Needs and Disabilities (SEND) or mental health needs.**
- **Small schools.**
- **Family pressures.**
- **Personal health.**
- **Changes to Initial Teacher Training.**

Governance

Governance of schools is a complex matter, as with all school-related work, it is very much dependent on building strong relationships based on clear communication and boundaries. I have been so blessed with some of the governors that have supported my leadership journey, but this did not happen by accident. I actively recruited professionals and members of the community who I believed would bring a range of strengths and different perspectives to the team. When I was a deputy head in a large primary school, I asked to join the governor meetings as an observer and my head of school was really obliging – I learnt so much from him about how to keep the key governors involved and use their strengths. I will always be grateful for this, as I make no bones about the fact that the first time I attended a governor meeting as a new head teacher, I felt like I was sitting in one of the parish council meetings on the Vicar of Dibley. (Apologies to the governors on that board who were brilliant and stuck with us)

Recruiting governors can be incredibly hard, and colleague heads will tell me that they don't remember the last time that they had a full complement of them. Who can blame people for not wanting to be a governor? It is a serious role, with lots of responsibility, little thanks and no financial reward. I personally have come across people who became governors for the wrong reasons and have been told many a story of how these ones can 'go rogue' if their responsibilities and obligations are not made clear from the outset. The most inspirational governor that I had the pleasure of working with for a few years had no personal connection to the school I led, but he had a passion to support our local community. When things got tough, he was grounded and diplomatic in his approach because he could keep his emotions under control and look at the whole picture. No wonder he has now gone on to be a brilliant Member of Parliament (MP) (and I say this genuinely with no hint of sarcasm). I actually think that he is a fine example of a compassionate leader, and I say that about very few politicians.

Specialist support

We could all talk for hours (even days) about our experiences with the lack of specialist support available to our young people. I have not met many leaders who don't want an inclusive school and want nothing more than to be able to meet all the needs of their pupils, but there are some major hindrances to this. With referral and assessment processes being staggeringly long and issues with recruiting the most suitable staff to work with those young people, schools are often unable to meet their needs. This is a subject I cannot cover with enough depth in this book, and there are SEND specialists out there raising awareness of this in their work – I extend gratitude and thanks to them and hope that change is coming.

I have recently trained as a performance coach, and many of my clients are working in education in one form or another. The very clear picture is of a profession which barely keeps its head above water. Clients talk about their love of the art of teaching, building relationships and inspiring great learning. However, they also report that they feel that they have no autonomy in their classrooms; they are bound by zero tolerance behaviour models and accountability systems created by their leaders to satisfy Ofsted judgements. Whether they are teachers or senior leaders, the real fear around inspections is a key reason why people want to leave the profession. If you add into this the excessive hours that school staff are working, both in and out of school, the endless paperwork, the parental complaints, lack of funding for basic resources and the issues that schools have with attendance post-pandemic, it's no wonder teachers are struggling. There are many other jobs that at times seem much more appealing.

It is still a wonderful and rewarding profession

Despite my own negative health experiences, I still maintain that teaching is a wonderful profession, leading a school is a great privilege and doing both these things well is a feeling like no other. We need to support and encourage people to train to be teachers and to *stay in* the role. We also need our middle leaders to look at headship and aspire to it – not run a mile in the other direction. Right now, both of those ideas seem like complete fantasy, and here I am no longer in post telling you what should be happening! It hasn't always been like this – yes teaching and leadership have always been tough, but overall, the positive days kept us all going. Now we have less and less of those days and more and more of the 'wading through treacle with concrete shoes on' kind of days.

Total transformation or more sticking plasters?

There are many other reports and anecdotes from school staff that I could include in this chapter, however what we need to do is concentrate on repairing our broken system and decide whether it is time for total transformational change or more educational sticking plasters. How do we do this and keep our excellent staff in school and our students learning? How do we encourage the next generation of teachers to stick around? Are the hard leadership strategies being used by leaders working for the system, or do we need to reframe our intentions and keep ourselves well at the same time? It is a real paradox that needs further examination.

Change is needed across all levels of school, but my argument is that it needs to start with leaders and those who mentor and train the leaders of tomorrow.

Using personal experiences to make changes

I was a newly qualified teacher at the age of 30, I had two small children and most of my support came from my parents. The head teacher of my first school was a 'headmistress' in many senses of the word – she did not allow time off during the school day for medical appointments, you were not paid if you took time off to look after your sick children and going to see them in any type of show or sporting activity was never authorised. I have no memories of taking either of my daughters to their first day at school as it was their grandparents who did this for me – something that will always make me sad.

So, what do you think I did when I became a head teacher?

Of course, I allowed my staff to do all the above; they were not financially penalised, and I often covered their classes myself. Did this make me a weak leader, or did it strengthen the relationships I had with my staff and increase their sense of belonging to a community that cared about them? If at this point you are thinking that they were not the right leadership decisions to make, I challenge you not to put the book down but to carry on reading and see if I can influence your way of viewing leadership. I am obviously not the only leader who puts their staff first, and you can read many brilliant leadership books and blogs on this very subject.

Being kind does not make you weak.

The rest of this book will focus on the changes that the profession can make to support schools to turn the trajectory of negativity into schools that thrive. I will examine the work of great leaders and the research behind them. I will highlight what really matters in leadership and life, and how we can create schools with a culture of compassion and authenticity – where people are always put first. It will help us as leaders regain our perspective, realign our values and recognise the possibilities that are out there.

The Dalai Lama, leader of the Tibetan People, has a wonderful way of capturing the key difference between empathy and compassion.

> Empathy is to raise your consciousness of the other. Compassion is to work with that knowledge with positive intent.

Take a moment:

- For a moment I want you to remember (if you can) a leader who had a positive impact on you as a teacher. They do not have to be a head teacher; they could be a head of department, or an older more experienced teacher or your Initial Teacher Training (ITT) mentor. Then remember a leader whom you have met who had a negative impact on you or left you wondering if your values were aligned.
- Make a list of what made them so different from each other; you will have learnt valuable lessons from both, but you will have learnt about the leader you wish to be from only one of them.

Bibliography

The Teacher Wellbeing Index 2023 https://www.educationsupport.org.uk/media/0h4jd5pt/twix_2023.pdf.

The Headrest Annual Report 2023 https://www.headrestuk.co.uk/blog/headteacher-wellbeing-report-2023.

Winnicott, D. (1962) *The Child and the Family: First Relationships.* London Tavistock.

Compassionate leadership and why it matters – be brave, not brutal

This chapter will explore the ideas that

- Schools need more focus on soft leadership skills, and leaders need to be clear which ones are appropriate in their different contexts.
- Soft leadership skills work more effectively due to the human element of school settings.

Jacinda Ardern highlights the importance of compassion in leadership in her autobiography:

> One of the criticisms I've faced over the years is that I'm not aggressive enough or assertive enough or, somehow because I'm empathetic, it means I am weak. I totally rebel against that. I refuse to believe that you cannot be both compassionate and strong.

Recent changes in our perception of leadership

In today's ever-changing workplace, leadership has been undergoing a seismic change, and the world of education is playing catch up (aren't we always?). According to a recent report in Psychology Today, 'The future belongs to leaders who embrace compassion, inclusivity and emotional intelligence'.

Whilst we all know leaders in schools who do this well, we have also all heard of or worked in establishments where kindness and compassion has been replaced by non-negotiables and rigid behaviour systems which are not inclusive of all staff, let alone pupils. In the past, kindness has been seen as a weakness, a failure to make big decisions or an unwillingness to initiate the clear and courageous conversations that need to be had – but there are signs that things are changing. In the report, 'Beyond Ofsted: Inquiry into the Future of School Inspection', James Knight includes in the foreward a snapshot of the changes that could be considered, not just to the inspection system but to the school system as a whole. He describes the fact that the teaching professions and parents have lost their trust in Ofsted and those relationships need to be repaired. He puts forward two options:

1. To get rid of single-word judgements and add in more regular safeguarding checks – both suggestions were initially rejected by the Department for Education (DFE), but in September 2024 the overall single-word judgement was removed from reports. Interestingly, despite this, there is little or no difference in how some schools are using the new system to advertise and promote that they are better than others. Many school leaders would agree with me that this is not a healthy or progressive way to support the education system from their place within it.

2. Begin total transformational change, based on some of the systems in the international school system.

   - Introduce the strategy of schools having a long-term relationship with an external assessor, which will aim to build relationships with the leaders, and drive school improvement in partnership with them.
   - The partners and their team would spend time learning about the school context, what makes it unique and what its biggest challenges are.
   - The partners will then produce real-time and transparent reports about the school outcomes and progress from those starting points.
   - These partners will regularly engage with the school community around its curriculum and pedagogy, and support the school leaders to develop an action plan that fits the school and the resources available to it.

I have purposely used the term 'partner' multiple times to change the perspective from passive to active engagement, identifying a system where there is real, honest partnership work to ensure school improvement and good outcomes for pupils.

The changes mooted in option 2 would mean that the 'hard leadership' focus on satisfying the rigours of a very rigid and high-pressure inspection, and the use of phrases like 'non-negotiables', could be morphed into something 'softer' and more suited to the context of a school system centred around human relationships. The possibilities for school improvement can then be built upon the individual needs of the school, and not upon a box-filling methodology devised by someone who is not an expert in this school.

So, what are these 'soft leadership' skills?

Where have they come from and why do they work in a school context?

If you research the term on your preferred internet search engine, you will get a plethora of information about 'soft leadership' and how it works in business; there is less information on its success in the education sector. Is this because it implies a lack of substance, application or necessity? Some evidence suggests that the term 'Soft Leadership' originated in the US military over 50 years ago, although I am sure there will be other sources that say otherwise. Initially, the term 'Soft Leadership Skills' was used to differentiate those key interpersonal and thinking skills, from the more technical proficiencies that can often be necessary in leadership generically. The term 'Soft Leadership' can have quite negative connotations in the world of education, which seems ironic, as it is so well known and used in the military. There are articles on the 'Top 10, Top 5' most used and even 'The 11C's of soft leadership', and all are very much worth a read. It seems to me that these skills are the ones that highly effective school leaders use in abundance; some come quite naturally, and others require a conscious change of habits and perspective.

Here are the most commonly occurring ones:

Communication	Emotional intelligence	Adaptability
Creativity	Decision-making	Project management
Problem-solving	Management	Conflict resolution
Teamwork	Interpersonal communication	Critical thinking
Delegation	Active listening	Motivation
Coaching	Confidence	Collaboration
Learning	Negotiation	Persuasion
Empathy	Time management	Flexibility
Compassion	Authenticity	

There are too many of these skills in the table above, and we need to identify those that have the most positive impact on school leadership. Many leadership experts would identify that the most effective leaders have **empathy, compassion** and **authenticity**. We will all have slightly different ideas about these skills and may even want to change those identified in the table above. With further consideration, and briefly, what I am describing is leadership that is kind. Leaders who are kind to their community, and to themselves, can be incredibly successful.

In an article in *Forbes Magazine*, Robert Logeman (January 2023) describes 'soft skills as hard currency in the workplace'. In the World's Economic Forum List, they have named the top 15 Workforce Skills for 2025 – these are some that I have chosen from that list, that I believe school leaders who are effective do well.

- Active learning and learning strategies.

- Critical thinking and analysis.

- Creativity, originality and initiative.
- Leadership and social influence.
- Resilience, stress tolerance and flexibility.
- Emotional intelligence.
- Persuasion and negotiation.

Take a moment:

- **Look at the skills listed above and note down how you use them at work.**
- **Think about the ones you would like to do more of and why.**

Empathy

It is generally recognised that empathy is when you not only understand another person's feelings but, to some extent, feel them too. It is deemed to be about attempting to see things from someone else's perspective, which in some cases will inspire you to take action to support or help them in some way. We discuss empathy time and time again in this book, so understanding what it is is essential.

Sadly, I have come across leaders that believe that empathy is well-meaning but unnecessary – this could not be further from the truth. In a recent conversation with a colleague, they told me about a head who asked a pregnant teacher how they were feeling, and when the teacher thanked her for being interested, she replied that she was only asking as it was her legal obligation to do so.

I cannot imagine a leader showing less empathy, can you?

What does empathetic leadership mean to you?

I believe, amongst other things, it is about respecting a team member's voice, life circumstances and their need to balance work and home. It is about taking the time to feel what another person feels, without allowing these feelings to overwhelm us; instead, using them to act. Compassion is often described as a social feeling that motivates people to go out of their way to relieve physical, mental or emotional pain of others and themselves; leadership through compassion means making those intentional connections to foster understanding and inclusion.

Where does emotional intelligence fit in?

Emotional intelligence is often described as the ability to recognise and manage our own emotions and equally recognise and respond to others. In 1998, Daniel

Goleman created the five pillars of emotional intelligence, refining them to four in 2002:

1. Self-awareness.
2. Self-management.
3. Social awareness.
4. Relationship management.

- **Self-awareness**: Understanding your own emotions, thoughts and behaviours, and how they impact others.
- **Self-management**: The ability to regulate your emotions and actions in a constructive way.
- **Social awareness**: Recognising and understanding the emotions of others, including their perspectives and social cues.
- **Relationship management**: Building and maintaining positive relationships by effectively managing interactions with others.

Goleman's model puts each of these in a section of the quadrant and develops them further. It is an interesting read and made me consider how and why children can find empathy so challenging when there is so much involved in it. According to John Mayer (University of New Hampshire) and one of the pioneers of the understanding on emotional intelligence, self-awareness is 'being aware of both our mood and our thoughts about our mood' (Salovey & Mayer, 1990, Original work published 1990). This is the notion of not just saying 'I feel so fed up' but being able to think about why you feel this way. The argument is that the more aware we are of our emotions in that moment, the easier they become for us not only to manage but also to shape how we might respond to others.

There is a school of thought which proposes that you can improve your emotional awareness if you work on a sequence like the one underneath.

1. Sense the emotion or feeling.
2. Acknowledge that it is there and do not ignore it.
3. Take a moment to reflect on why it would be there.
4. Accept the emotion.
5. Take appropriate action based on your acceptance of the emotion.
6. Reflect on the emotions and the action taken and decide what you learnt from it and whether you would change anything.

This entire process can be completed in minutes if you train yourself to notice things *before* you react. It certainly takes practice and is not something that my younger self knew how to do. Leaders who lead with compassion will be people who are aware of, and in tune with their emotions, and how their reactions will affect others.

We generally understand *social awareness* as being able to firstly notice the emotions of others and then having the ability to try to recognise why they are there. In leadership positions that require daily involvement with other people, we must try and 'read' situations appropriately. School leaders often walk into classrooms in which an event has already occurred, one in which both children and adults are dysregulated; they will need to assess the differing emotions on display and the varying perspectives of that event. Meetings with families and members of staff can be made harder if we are not able to at least try and sense what others may be thinking or feeling. You will recognise the fact that we often sit in meetings which begin with everyone only recognising their own emotions and no else's. This is completely natural human behaviour, but it must be someone's role to try and engender an awareness that recognises them all and can offer a practical solution to move things forward. Goleman explains that this ability to 'read' others comes from neurons in our extended circuitry which is connected to the amygdala. Your brain circuitry sends you information from the conversations you are having such as:

> He is getting angry with me – it must have been what I just said.
> They are looking really tired – maybe they are bored, or they didn't sleep well last night.

We then use these messages to decide how we respond to them. It is no wonder that after difficult meetings or behaviour incidents we are exhausted; if we are trying to deal with a situation with compassion and kindness, it means a lot of processing going on behind the scenes (in our brains!). These are the situations where we really listen, and not just listen to respond.

If you are self-aware and socially aware, and can on most occasions manage your own emotions, then this puts you in an ideal position to practice the skill of relationship management in both your professional and personal life. Relationship management can be used effectively to support your team, to make effective decisions and to mediate the conflict of others, whether they are children or adults. In many cases of conflict in the workplace, the issues are often caused by the delivery and tone of an instruction/direction rather than the instruction/direction itself.

A book that impacted my emotional intelligence significantly is **The Chimp Paradox – The Mind Managment: Programme for Confidence, Success, and Happiness by Dr. Steve Peters**. It helped me to recognise that my own emotions could often be hijacked, and that difficult conversations needed to be prepared for, by trying to consider the emotions of the other people involved. Dr. Peters has worked in the field of psychiatry for decades and holds numerous degrees and qualifications; he has worked with elite sportspeople and chief executive officers

(CEOs) and is far more qualified than me to explain his programme. However, I will try to give you some insights, as it relates so well to leadership, stress and how we communicate. The book was first published in 2011, and I attended a conference where Dr. Peters spoke a year or so later. I was subsequently lucky enough to be part of the leadership training that was rolled out to Isle of Wight leaders. I still refer to the book regularly and it is full of my scribbles and Post-it notes – a clear sign that it is well worth a read.

The Chimp Paradox is a way of simplifying the science of how our brains work and how this is linked to our emotions. Within this model, the brain has three sections – frontal, limbic and parietal – and they together form what is known as the 'Psychological Mind'. As Dr. Peters states on the very first page, 'scientifically this is far from accurate, but it will give us a working model'.

For people like me, who are fascinated by human behaviour, this model is perfect for looking beyond the science and directly into behaviours instead. Within the model, the frontal lobe is referred to as *the human*, the limbic as *the chimp* and the parietal as *the computer*. For our purpose, we need only think about the roles of the human and the chimp, particularly when it comes to understanding communicating with empathy, courage and compassion. We will return to them in more detail further on in the book and look at the value of recognising how we process and respond to different situations. But firstly, it is useful to understand why applied emotional intelligence in education is so vital.

So, if we lose the term 'soft skills' and instead think of compassionate leadership, let us ask the question: **Why is compassionate leadership so effective in school settings, and why isn't it used more?**

The link between soft skills and the school environment

Schools are made up of a mix of ingredients, but the biggest one is quite simply human beings. Schools are full of people. From the child who has just turned four in August, to the school governor who has just had their 70th birthday, we are dealing with people on a day-to-day, hour-to-hour, minute-to-minute basis. If your job involves the leadership of people, then surely, kindness, compassion, empathy and authenticity must play a significant role in what you do. Imagine a school that does not think relationships are important. One that believes non-negotiables, tick boxes, following fixed procedures and policies and putting people (big and small) in boxes is the only way to be successful. Sadly, many of you will not just be imagining a school like this but are in fact working in one.

I cannot stress enough that relationships are the key to successful schools and leaders who recognise and promote this are inspirational – we need to keep those leaders in place.

A kind leader has model integrity at every opportunity and sticks to the principles of compassion and authenticity. If the school culture is one of kindness, then direct and difficult conversations can be had within a coaching, supportive environment.

Compassionate leadership in business – Brene Brown and Simon Sinek

Brene Brown describes this in business terms in her book *Dare to Lead*, clearly stating that 'avoiding difficult conversations is not kind' (2018). The theory in much of her writing, which can be directly applied to schools, is that leaders need to be braver in the conversations that they have, as giving honest and productive feedback is kinder than being unclear about what you need staff to do and how to behave. Communicating with clarity and understanding is more effective and more respectful, and nourishes relationships.

In his 2011 book, *Start with Why. How Great Leaders Inspire Everyone to Take Action*, Simon Sinek does exactly this – he looks forensically at great leaders and how they managed to inspire followers when others did not. Like many books about leadership, this is based on the global business sector, but once again, the principles of leadership can be used effectively in the global education system. When reading Sinek's book, and watching his TED Talks, one of the standout factors for me was his ability to tell a story, to really get 'under the skin' of the person or company he is describing. As educators, we know the power of stories yet sometimes shy away from talking about lived experiences and human connection when leading change and try to rely on data and statistics instead. Yet with a combination of narrative and data/statistics that support the same theory, you can co-construct a transformative, powerful and persuasive dialogue. Sinek's simple theory, that has resonated across the world, is that the leaders who inspire us most are the ones that communicate with you their 'why'. If you know someone's why, and it speaks to you in a positive way, then this can prompt you to take action too. This is the opposite of simply being blindly compliant with your leader's goals – you act because you want to, because you see the point and understand the purpose. I highly recommend that if you have not taken time to dip your toes into the work of Simon Sinek, you should. In all his work, he refers to a 'Golden Circle' which contains the words why, how and what – why is in the centre. In a nutshell, as humans we buy into the why – we buy into a person's or a business's or a school's values, in other words its purpose. We look at this in more detail in Chapter 4 when we discuss why culture is so important to a community.

I can relate to Sinek's theory in terms of my own leadership journey experiences (I really do not like using the word journey, but have yet to find a satisfactory alternative.). In the first few years of my headship, I was determined to prove that the team around me could be improved with my support and encouragement, particularly in terms of their own autonomy; but at times I omitted to communicate to them what the school as a whole needed and what my overall vision for it was – in plain terms, the 'why' was sometimes missing. As a brand new head, I had, of course, imparted my opening gambits, during initial In-service training (INSET) days and staff meetings, announcing what I believed in, but beyond that, I did not give myself or my colleagues enough time to see if they shared the same core values as me – the open and direct dialogue should have continued. Consequently, over time, I realised that we were not always aligned, and I had to be much clearer in my conversations with them, in terms of expectations for the good of the children and in the long term to be kinder to them. I now know that creating a culture in any environment takes time, energy and unrelenting consistent focus on acting in a way that models what you want from every member of staff. It is exhausting, but when it starts to show in others, it is worth every effort.

So, what is it about compassionate leadership that really works in business and can be transferred into the world of education?

There is no science behind the idea that kindness makes you weak; in fact studies and workplace questionnaires show that it is kind leaders whom we want to work for. Jacinda Ardern showed the world that it is possible to lead with empathy, to put people first and still win. She found that the more compassionate and generous she was, the more people gravitated to support the outcomes that she was passionate about.

Behind every member of your team and school community is their *why*, leaders need to be curious about these, explore them and use them to create a unified and cohesive team based on common values. If you are a head teacher who is new to a setting, using the work of Sinek to draw information from your team about what led them to teaching and what are their own plans and aspirations is an effective way to begin your professional relationship with them. It gives you an insight into their own values, their personal experiences of education and their future goals. I would argue that this is more powerful than a spreadsheet of their previous performance management targets or lesson observation reports.

It is a sad fact that people leave their jobs due to a lack of support from leaders, or lack of connection with their boss, whilst working for a kind leader has been shown to increase morale and decrease absenteeism. Simon Sinek in his book *Leaders Eat Last. Why Some Teams Pull Together and Others Don't* (2019) claims that working in an environment with a kind leader who promotes psychological safety can prolong the lives of their employees by decreasing their stress levels. This is a bold claim, but when you align it with the staggering statistics on what causes burnout (particularly in education), you can clearly see the correlations. About 84% of senior leaders who responded to the current Teacher Wellbeing Index (2024) reported that they were stressed, and 50% of all staff said that the culture of their school or college had a negative impact on their mental health and well-being.

A kind and compassionate leader can still make tough decisions and drive results, as being kind is vastly different from just being nice. There are, of course, overlaps in both qualities, but being nice can be counterproductive and stop you from having the clear and courageous conversations that are often needed – because it makes you feel guilty. If you think of these conversations as necessary, then prepare for them appropriately. At some point in your experience, you will develop the belief that tackling difficult discussions head on, with kindness and authenticity, is more effective – both during the discussions themselves and in the long term. There are some examples of this further on in the book.

Engendering morale

Businesses with kind and compassionate leaders, who actively and positively engage with their staff, are more likely to build a strong team with higher morale, and morale is something that needs urgent attention in our schools. Good schools run on good will (rightly or wrongly), and if you successfully create a culture in which your staff know that they can talk to you and be listened to, and have time off for life events and be supported in their career development, you will have a team willing to go the extra mile for the good of the pupils.

And this brings us back to empathy. This is a skill that takes practice and is not just a checklist of listening with your eyes and your ears and using helpful body language, although this would be a good starting point. We cannot understand or appreciate anyone else's point of view without taking time to communicate, ask them questions and actively and openly listen to their answers, without attaching our own biases to them. These are the kind of skills effective coaches have. Active listening means really tuning into what they are saying, stop thinking about the clever thing that you are going to answer with and connect with this person on a deeper level. After you have done this, it is the appropriate time to offer your perspective and support. Alan Alda writes in his book, *Never Have Your Dog Stuffed: And Other Things I've Learned (2006),* 'Real listening is a willingness to let the other person change you'. If you do not take the time to listen to your staff and really talk to them, then the alternative is that they will talk *about* you and your lack of interest in them, and this is how a toxic culture can start to germinate.

Common purpose unites a team

Manley Hopkinson (not the poet) is an explorer, author and a leading voice in the field of leadership, and you can find him on his website, Manley Talks. In his book *Compassionate Leadership: How to Create and Maintain Engaged, Committed and High-Performing Teams* (2014), he discusses how to encourage your team to work together in a meaningful way and how important it is to have a common purpose and goal – in the same way schools have their vision. In his many podcasts and interviews, he has a phrase that I absolutely adore and that is to be able to lead with compassion; the first thing you must do is 'Shut up and listen'. So simple, yet so true!

I had the pleasure of talking to Manley after connecting with him on social media, and he was incredibly generous with his time and expertise. His experiences in leadership include skippering a yacht in the world's toughest race, the

BT Global Challenge, and competing in a race for the North Pole, and although those experiences differ from my own, there are still many things that connect our views about leading with compassion – we certainly believe in the same values and behaviours. Perhaps, if he spent a wet Friday afternoon in a reception class with no teaching assistant, he would get a different sort of insight into challenge. (This is, of course, a joke Manley, if you are reading this!)

In both our worlds, the importance of a team with a collective purpose is central.

> The big impact of compassionate leadership is to create what I call Collective Brilliance.
>
> (Hopkinson, 2014)

A strong team will be united not only by common purpose but also by the feeling of shared success. Honest, open leadership with a holistic approach can result in a workforce where every individual feels they contribute to the successes, that they have been part of the process and that their efforts have value. Hopkinson describes this as 'whole team development' (2014).

Take a moment:

- **Can you remember the last time you felt that someone had really listened to you?**
- **When was the last time you put everything to one side and really listened to someone who needed you to?**

The importance of being authentic

Let me give you an example.
  Imagine this scenario:
You have a class where there are a small number of parents who are quick to complain about things (as is their right) and this year that class has a second year Early Career Teacher (ECT) teacher. It is not long before a parent makes a complaint about the teacher, and it is allegedly about how that member of staff spoke to their child and blamed them for something that the child claims they had nothing to do with (sounding familiar?). As the head teacher, because you have the context of this parent and know of complaints that have happened previously that have come to nothing, your first thought might be to protect your member of staff – after all they have enough to think about. You then try to investigate the allegation by talking to the teaching assistant in the classroom and the children involved, but not the teacher.

  Why would this not be the best way to deal with this situation?
  Although you know that the teacher will be upset about the complaint, it is always better to tell them about it yourself. Otherwise, that teacher will see you

talking to their teaching assistant and pupils and know that something is wrong. They could assume that they are the problem and will imagine it is much worse than it actually is. The stress that the teacher will feel will be much worse than if you sit down and are honest about the situation and hear their perspective before anyone else's. This will show that you trust your staff and are willing to support them in these situations. Creeping around trying to find out information, even with good intentions, will not result in positive outcomes.

One of the key indicators of a kind leader is that they are authentic. This means, amongst other things, that they are self-aware, sincere, thoughtful and open to feedback. Authentic leaders are always honest about what may be happening within the school's context; they share the decisions that are made and explain the reasoning behind them. If you work in a school with an authentic leader, then you should not be highjacked by 'quick fix decisions' as you will have been informed every step of the way about the process. Some leaders would counter this, by arguing that it is a more effective strategy to not disclose in detail the changing nature of things from your team, because it will shelter them from the 'burden' of difficult decisions and problematic processes. However, by doing this, you are metaphorically 'keeping them in the dark', creating an unsettling environment within which it can be quite natural for staff to form their own imaginary scenarios and share them with others, causing unnecessary stress for everyone involved. Ideally, the staff in your school will be driven by the same purpose and values as you, and within an environment of transparency and trust they will recognise the logic behind decisions that are made. Leading schools is tough but being open and honest about the challenges you are facing can only make your team stronger and more loyal to the culture that you have built. Authenticity requires building trust and having clear communication systems, especially around work expectations and goals; this, in turn, means being transparent about your vision and needs, as well as your personal drivers. Whilst I am not advocating that you share every little concern that you have as a school leader, or every emotion that you are feeling, as this would just turn you into a world-class whiner, but being honest about the things that really matter to the whole school community bonds you to your team.

Be authentic about the big stuff, positive and negative, and people will have a better understanding of decisions that have been made, even if, ultimately, they do not like them.

An authentic leader will always celebrate the growth and successes of their team, and not hold them back, but robust leadership also means sometimes undertaking tough discussions. As Brene Brown advocates (2018), have difficult conversations at the appropriate time. It is important that those tricky conversations are had with compassion, empathy and clarity; if you work in a culture of trust, then your team will grow from any potentially difficult feedback and see it as a development point rather than a criticism. Only toxic cultures hold back honest and open conversations.

Take a moment:

- Can you think of a time when someone showed empathy towards you in a workplace situation? How did they do it and how did it make you feel?

- Can you think of a time when someone was *not* empathetic towards you in a workplace situation? How did they do it and how did it make you feel?

Bibliography

Alda, A. (2006) *Never Have Your Dog Stuffed, and Other Things I Have Learnt.* Random House Inc, US.

Brown, B. (2018) *Dare to Lead: Brave Work, Tough Conversations, Whole Hearts.* Vermillion.

Goleman, D. (2007) *Emotional Intelligence.* Bantum Books.

Hopkinson, M. (2022) *Compassionate Leadership.* Little Brown.

Logeman, R. (10 January 2023) *How Strong Are Your Leadership Soft Skills?* Forbes Magazine.

Peters, S. P. Dr. (2015) *The Chimp Paradox: The Science of Mind Management for Confidence, Success and Happiness.* Penguin Random House.

Salovey, P. & Mayer, J. D. (1990) Emotional Intelligence. *Imagination, Cognition and Personality*, 9(3), 185–211. https://doi.org/10.2190/DUGG-P24E-52WK-6CDG

Sinek, S. (2011) *Start with Why: How Great Leaders Inspire Everyone to Take Action.* Penguin US.

Sinek, S. (2019) *Leaders Eat Last: Why Some Teams Pull Together and Others Don't.* Penguin Random House.

Supirnya, V. & Harte, C. A. (2021) *Jacinda Adern: Leading with Empathy.* One World Publications.

Well-being strategies to avoid burnout and keep your community positive

This chapter will explore the ideas that

- Burnout is a real and dangerous phenomenon, but it can be avoided.
- Managing workload is key to your well-being.
- Picking your battles is a game changer in leadership and in life.

What is burnout?

Despite the prevalence of burnout in many professions, it is still not classified as a medical or mental health condition. The World Health Organisation describes it simply as a condition – a collection of symptoms or signs associated with a specific health-related cause (Mental Health UK). It describes burnout as an 'occupational phenomenon'. It is recognised as a syndrome, conceptualised as resulting from chronic workplace stress that has not been successfully managed. Psychologists say that there are three main dimensions that indicate you are in the state of burnout and these are:

1. **Feelings of emotional, mental and physical exhaustion.**
2. **Increased mental distancing from your job role.**
3. **Feelings of negativity or cynicism about your job role and your workplace.**

These, of course, are overly simplistic descriptions of the totally devastating effects that burnout can have on you both physically and mentally. Educators that I have spoken with about their own experiences have used the following terms to describe just some of the ways it left them feeling.

> I felt completely helpless and unable to fulfil my role, either at home or school.
> I was overwhelmed with feelings of self-doubt and failure.
> I felt alone and unsupported and often thought that I would be better off dead.

DOI: 10.4324/9781003558088-4

As in my case, burnout often leads to people having a full mental health crisis, a term that is now used instead of nervous breakdown. The journey back to wellness after this is long and difficult, and what we need is to be able to recognise where our stress levels are taking us before we get to this place.

The latest Teacher Wellbeing Report issues a stark warning about stress and the levels of burnout within the profession.

Percentages of people suffering with symptoms of burnout:

Teachers – 37% up by 9%

Leaders – 40% up by 3%

Support staff – 29% up by 8%

Personally, I have experienced burnout twice during the 13 years that I was a serving head teacher and I firmly believe that with the right support and education regarding this phenomenon it could have been avoided on both occasions (hindsight is a wonderful thing I know). It is important to be aware at this point that I have had a relatively recent diagnosis of attention-deficit/hyperactivity disorder (ADHD), and those of us with this condition can often be more susceptible to burnout due to differing factors. Of course, many of you reading this could also have a diagnosis or suspect that you too are neurodivergent.

The first occasion was shortly before the first COVID-19 lockdown, and I will never forget the feelings of failure associated with the fact that I had to be signed off work and leave my leadership team to deal with the implications of the lockdown. Of course, this is what a good and effective leadership team is trained to do, but the negative spiral that I was in just exacerbated the mental health crisis that I was struggling with. I have many times tried to unpick the exact thing that made me so stressed during this period of headship, and, of course, the role is far too complex to be able to identify the minutiae of events. I do recognise, however, that at this point I was dealing with an exceedingly difficult family whose complaints had resulted in them reporting me to the police for a string of fabricated claims. Whilst nothing came of these complaints, the entire process was long, stressful and incredibly disempowering. Maintaining your integrity and keeping a dignified silence when others are free to post their views and accusations on social media and discuss their opinions of you with all and sundry is a hard rock to find yourself under. I know that many of you will have found yourself having similar experiences, and I have every sympathy for you.

Challenging conversations and difficult parent or carer relationships are common to the role of leaders in schools, but sometimes these do escalate to an altogether different level, and it is at those times that you need to be supported. A head teacher can often spend so much time and energy protecting their staff from these elements, that they are left dealing with them in isolation. This is where clear policies and systems need to be in place for your own protection. Don't put these in place after the event – make sure they are watertight before your very first day in the role.

Policies for communication

In terms of effective policies to support and protect your staff and yourself, it is always vital to have a complaints policy that works – it needs to be set out in stages, with clear steps for the complainant to follow and with timeframes that you need to stick to. Furthermore, it also needs to be clear enough for your governing body or trust members to follow as they will be dealing with most complaints after a certain stage in the process. This may sound obvious, but I was caught out by this in my first year of headship as the policy had not been updated as it was still in date and seemingly fit for purpose. There was nowhere near enough clarity in the policy, and it paid no attention to vexatious complainers and how long a single complaint could run on for. Granted this was 15 years ago, but please ensure that your policy is fit for purpose.

I also think there is a need if not for a policy but at the very least for a 'code of practice' in how meetings with staff and parents should be conducted. As with your behaviour policy, it is better to keep this positively framed and talk about expectations rather than the more negatively worded statements such as 'do not swear' and 'do not raise your voice'. Language is always a key element in these documents, emphasising a wish to resolve matters but in an appropriate way. Some schools prefer to have an overarching policy regarding communication in general; this will also hold your staff to account so please ensure that what you include in the policy is workable for busy teachers and office staff too. The Department for Education (DFE) website is a good starting point and aims to support schools to get these policies and practices right and highlights what your legal obligations are and what constitutes 'good practice'. If you are the leader in a small school and policy writing is down to you, which is still very common, ensure that you get someone to advise you on these essential ones. After my first formal complaint using the school's original policy, a consultant colleague wrote a watertight version that ensured the process was equitable for all parties moving forward. The best part of this was it meant that most complaints could be dealt with at the early stages of the process and therefore cut down on work and extra stress for key members of staff.

My second experience of burnout I have described in the preface of this book, and whilst I don't want to dwell on negative experiences, I think it is important that if you are a leader reading this book, you can begin to recognise if you too are in danger of burnout. If you recognise any of the following emotions, then maybe it is time to stop and think about what you are going to do to manage your own well-being.

- **Do you feel like you have been carrying too much for too long?**
- **Do you think that you are losing your empathy for others?**
- **Do you feel that nothing you do makes any difference anyway?**

The reality for people working in caring professions is that we can begin to suffer with something called 'Compassion Fatigue', and as the entire premise of this book is that we need compassionate leaders, we really must ensure that we don't start to lose this because of the enormity and complexity of our jobs. Emotional exhaustion can have the most negative impact on our health, and, of course, it is impossible to work in schools and not feel a range of emotions on a daily, if not hourly basis.

What is stress and why is it so damaging?

Before moving on to what we can do to protect our own health both physically and emotionally, it is important that we understand exactly what stress is, what it can do to our bodies and why it is vital that we are able to return our physical states back to normal after experiencing stressful episodes. A simplistic definition of stress is that it is a state of worry or mental tension caused by a difficult situation. What this definition doesn't tell us is the physical effects stress can have on our bodies. We know that stress can trigger our parasympathetic reactions of fight, flight or freeze. If we opt for the fight response, it means we are motivated to approach the situation and respond with only our first instincts in control. If we choose flight, it means we want to avoid all responses and get as far away as possible and choosing freeze takes us to a response that our ancestors would have called 'playing dead'. They all have advantages and disadvantages, but the important thing to remember is that we cannot stay in this response mode for long without it causing harm to our bodies and therein lies the problem with many of us.

If we do not close the stress cycle, we remain stuck in a state where our stress levels remain chronically activated.

Emily and Amelia Nagoski write extensively about this in their book *Burnout: The Secret to Solving the Stress Cycle* (2019). They are a fascinating case study, identical twins, one with a PhD in Health Behaviour and the other with PhD in Musical Arts. They argue that 'our lives are humming with stress, and we never complete the cycle' (Nagoski, 2019). In their book, they suggest seven coping strategies to reduce stress and help you to complete the cycle. In their words, 'Cracking this is the key to unlocking ourselves from our hyped-up cages and into mental clarity' (Nagoski, 2019). The twins have a theory that the moment your body recognises that it is safe from the danger (stress) it has been exposed to, then the cycle of stress is closed and complete.

One of the issues with stress in the workplace, and in modern life in general, is that we are unable to close the cycle, often because of our own actions.

Let me give you an example.

Imagine this scenario:

You are informed one evening whilst at home that a parent, or a group of parents, has been making negative remarks about your school on social media, this is something that would make your stress levels rise; consequently, your body will be automatically flooded with cortisol and adrenaline. This, in turn, will trigger a fight, flight or freeze response in you – just like it has in humans for thousands of years. In this instance, you are unlikely to do any of these things, but what you will do is scroll through your phone or laptop, trying to find related comments. You might check your emails and see if anything has been sent to you or even contact the parents yourself via email.

Why is this not the most appropriate reaction if we are considering our well-being?

These actions do not complete the stress cycle; they will only ever make it worse. In fact, in our busy work lives, we will probably have situations like this several times a day, and so our stress response becomes chronically activated; this, in turn, will send our blood pressure soaring, putting us at serious risk of heart disease (this is sounding remarkably familiar to me!). So, it seems to me that the Nagoski sisters are spot on with their theory, and it is true that if you do not complete the stress cycle, then you are putting your mental and physical health under significant strain and ultimately risking your life.

How can we keep our stress levels down?

If you have read this book or listened to any of the interviews with both Emily and Amelia, you will be aware that for them, three is not the magic number, but seven is. They recommend seven strategies that will help you to close your stress cycle and actively prevent you from burning out. They are as follows:

Activity	How and why!
Moving	This is not new to us! Exercise is always the first line of attack when dealing with stress but is often the least used (I include myself in this.). We should be aiming for a minimum of 20 minutes a day. Find something that you enjoy or can tolerate at least and try to do it as much as possible. Getting outdoors for a short walk is better than not doing anything at all.
Breathing	This seems obvious – but it is not as simple as it would first seem. This involves us adapting specific breathing techniques whilst feeling stressed. Any breathing that is long and slow is beneficial in these moments – you need to breathe so that you can feel your belly contract. One technique is to breathe in for 5 seconds, hold your breath for 5, exhale for 10 and then pause for a further 5. Repeat this three times or more and it will help to calm and close they cycle. There are many more like this, and you can find one that suits you.
Talking to people	Sometimes we let our stress build up inside us without sharing why we are feeling this way with anyone. We can seem perfectly fine and in control of a situation to others, but internally we are struggling. In my case, people always used to comment on how on top of things I was and how I was able to deal with difficult situations – I didn't share how difficult it was to keep this up.

Activity	How and why!
	To take our minds off this internal battle, the book recommends that we make conversation with the people around us – normal chit-chat with the person on the till in the supermarket or the barista in the coffee shop. You don't need to be telling them about your stress, but often just having normal interactions with people you don't really know on a personal level can subconsciously allow you to think that the world is a safe place after all.

Give it a try – if nothing else you will make someone happy that you have noticed them. |
| Laughing | This one really resonates with me personally as I know that it helps. However, at my most stressed moments and when I was in complete burnout, I would turn down invitations to meet up with people and attend events where I knew that I would have a good time, have fun and laugh with others. Sometimes we must push ourselves hard to take part, as stress can lead us to feel exhausted and totally unsociable. When we do manage to join in, it usually makes us feel a whole lot lighter – it closes the cycle.

'When we laugh', says neuroscientist Sophie Scott, 'we use an 'ancient evolutionary system that mammals have evolved to make and maintain social bonds and regulate emotions'. |
| Speaking to loved ones | There are times when the chit-chat mentioned above is not on its own enough to reduce your stress levels right down, and this is when you really need to talk to someone that you have a much deeper connection with.

I remember vividly a day in the run up to being signed off with stress that I went to talk to my dad. Telling him how I was feeling and sharing the level of the stress I was carrying was just what I needed – but I should have been doing it on a more regular basis and shouldn't have sat on it so long. My husband is also a teacher, and we used to talk regularly, even excessively about our jobs, but somehow, we both accepted that this constant feeling of stress and anxiety was just 'part of the job'.

There is a very good argument here for us to be having regular coaching/supervision sessions.

Someone who loves and respects you is in a unique position to help you close your cycle if you let them.

At some point during this conversation, make time for a hug – there is growing evidence from medical reports by organisations such as British United Provident Association (BUPA) that explain the benefits to health and well-being of a good, long hug (A 20 second hug infact). |

Activity	How and why!
	A good hug with someone you have a connection with can do the following things:

- Decrease your levels of cortisol which in turn will decrease your stress levels. This will also lower your blood pressure and improve your cardiovascular function. Instinctively, we know that this is true, but we haven't had the science to back it up before. What do so many (not all) dysregulated young people really need in that moment? Physical connection with someone they trust. This is one of the many reasons I struggle with schools that have a zero-contact policy – sometimes, it is essential.
- A hug can make you feel happier since it releases serotonin that in turn can you make you feel calmer and happier. Hugging can release the hormone oxytocin – often referred to as the 'love hormone'. Oxytocin is released during sex, birth and breastfeeding as well as in a warm, comfortable hug.
- The effects of a hug don't stop there – they can also reduce anxiety, relieve pain in the short term and reduce feelings of loneliness.
- Hugging one or both of my adult daughters is the biggest pleasure I can have.

It would be misguided of me to suggest that a hug is all you need or to recommend that we all start throwing our arms around anyone who comes to us with a problem. However, I am suggesting that you get to know who you can hug when you need one and who within your trusted circle would appreciate a hug in the right situation. It could make all the difference.

You can get all the same benefits from petting an animal if you are not a hugger. Find a friend with a labrador – they have more than enough love to go round.

Crying I believe that the progress that has been made in removing the stigma of crying making you weak is brilliant – but has it gone far enough? It would seem there are still lots of people who think that crying is a sign of your failure to cope and do not recognise it as a healthy coping mechanism.

The act of crying, and more importantly, getting it done and dusted, is an effective way of completing that circle of stress. The problem has not gone away at this point, but your emotional reaction to it at this juncture has very much done its job.

Activity	How and why!
Being creative	You don't have to be a degree level artist to enjoy spending time being creative. In an article in MQ – Mental Health Research, the benefits of creativity on our stress levels and overall mental health are explored. Whether it is painting, sculpting, knitting, journalling, baking and singing, it is proven that doing these things at the right time can close your cycle of stress. Art and music therapy are well used with inpatients with conditions such as depression, anxiety and schizophrenia. And in schools we use play therapy for many vulnerable young people. What does it do for us though? If we really get involved in a creative activity, something that needs us to think and focus on it, then we enter a sort of meditative flow which allows our brain to do some of the following: • Reframe perspectives. • Regulate emotions. • Become grounded in the present moment – rather than ruminating on the past or worrying about the future. As a head teacher, there were two things in my office that really helped pupils to calm down. One was huge box of Lego, and the other was a labrador called Betty.

The Nagoski sisters have given us some excellent advice in their book about closing the stress cycle, and I can see the sense in them – I hope you can too.

Should we have some stress in our lives?

It would be foolish to think that we can eradicate all stress from our lives, and as we know, it is good for us to have some stress to deal with. This kind of stress is called Eustress, and it is the kind of moderate stress that psychologists would consider to be good for us. The kind of tension that comes with reaching a goal, exercising, getting married or riding a rollercoaster releases endorphins into our system; this can have positive effects on our health, motivation and emotional well-being. This is the stress that people who play competitive sports need to perform to the best of their abilities. I always feel this kind of stress before and after facilitating a training session or keynote speaking in a room full of adults. Before the event, I always have a moment where I am close to the fight, flight or freeze reactions, but afterwards, when I have finished, and the session has gone well, the feeling is exhilarating, and this spurs me on to do it all again. After I come back down to earth, I then start to reflect and criticise myself for missing things out or not expanding on a good point or talking too fast – you get the point, don't you? The good stress feeling is fleeting, so enjoy it when you can. These are the moments that you can look back on when you are feeling that old imposter syndrome and remind yourself that you can be and often are bloody brilliant at what you do.

Take a moment:

- **When did you last do one of the seven strategies that are recommended by the sisters? Note down how it made you feel.**
- **Next time you are in the stress cycle pick one of the strategies and use it appropriately (try not to cry in the supermarket or hug a stranger for 20 seconds, unless, of course, you have their permission!).**

Managing workload to support your well-being

We have all been advised at some point in our working lives that managing our workload is the key to feeling less stress and being more efficient; but what does this mean, and what does it look like in reality? How do you sort out the stuff that makes a difference to your students from the stuff that is completely insignificant?

How many teachers up and down the country are told by their senior leaders to manage their workload better, knowing that much of the workload has been imposed on them by that actual team? In turn, the senior leaders will have had their workload increased by head teachers, executive head teachers, local authority school improvement teams and sometimes their own misplaced expectations of impending inspections.

When are we collectively going to come together and say enough is enough?

Ultimately, if you work in a school where workload and well-being are important, you will know it and feel it – and that comes down to the culture that has been created over time – not as the result of a quick fix.

Organisational culture is the biggest problem for more than half of the school workforce according to the Teacher's Wellbeing Index 2023.

Since leaving headship, I have had the absolute pleasure and privilege of visiting schools in a much wider vicinity than I ever could before. I am thoroughly enjoying the various roles that I am undertaking – coach, facilitator, personal tutor, speaker – and I am taking away so many nuggets of useful insight into how good schools work. I am now able to be a tiny part of what is happening for pupils aged 4 years old to 19+, and it has given me a whole new lease of my professional life – I'm learning again. What I am seeing in many schools fills me with hope that things are getting better, whilst also filling me with admiration for the leaders in schools who are building teams determined to make a difference to children's lives based on trust, compassion and coaching – a positive change from the top-down approach of leadership.

Schools who base their expectations of staff and pupils on the rigid Ofsted criteria, and not on what they know about their school community, are highly likely to be the schools where staff well-being is poor, and this relentless focus on inspection will only serve to ensure that it declines even further. As an educational professional, I am not saying that the inspection framework isn't important but what is *more* important is how well you (as a leader) know your context, how high you set your expectations (to ensure the best outcomes for your pupils) and how your staff feel about working in your school. The robust relationships that evolve through your coaching and the trust you have in your staff are elements that will get a school through any challenge – whether that is an inspection, poor results, the tragic loss of a member of the school community or any number of other things that can and do happen in an academic year.

Since starting to write this book, there have been some changes to the Ofsted framework, including the removal of an overall one-word judgement – too late for Ruth Perry and her loved ones, but it is there now all the same. Has it made a difference? In discussion with many colleague heads, it is seen as a starting point, but it isn't enough for meaningful change.

So, if you are not in the privileged position of creating and embedding the school culture and ethos of compassion and belonging, how do you protect your well-being by managing your own workload?

Where to begin with workload and well-being

A good start for teachers and leaders would be to treat yourself to a copy of 'Teacher Wellbeing & Self-Care' written by experts in the field, Adrian Bethune and Dr. Emma Kell. This book is part of the 'Little Guide for Teachers' series published by Sage. It is so easy to use for quick reference and full of practical tips. One thing I love about this book is that from the get-go (page 3 in fact) the authors define the fundamental nature of well-being and how it is innately linked to the essential satisfaction that we draw from our professional roles. We have all worked in settings, or heard about schools, where the focus on well-being is merely an add-on to the responsibilities of an already busy staff; ironically, it often gives them more to think about. You know what I am talking about – cakes on a Friday, compulsory socialising and free facials for support staff during teaching time. I have heard of some terrible ideas that may well have started from a place of support, and in many cases, it was a reaction to finding out that Ofsted will ask your staff about their workload and their well-being. Ultimately, a feeling of well-being comes from knowing you are doing your job well, and that all the effort you put in daily is worth it.

Time is of the essence

When I facilitate training in schools about reducing stress and improving well-being, one of the things I talk about is *time*. This may seem obvious, but you have 24 hours each day, and generally, this is divided into the following sections – sleep, work, family and leisure. Imagine a pie chart with these sections and consider whether your four sections would be equal. I am guessing that if you take into account the work you do at weekends and evenings, then your work section is bigger than the others. If more things are added to your workload, then where are you going to take that time from? Are you going to sleep less? Will you see your children or parents less frequently. Or accept that you will have no time at all to enjoy the occasional walk or trip to the cinema. When someone asks you to do extra, be brave enough to ask them what they are going to take away from you so that you can do it. Practice using a phrase like 'that doesn't work for me because of…'. It is also good practice to ask *why* you are being asked to do it – if it cannot be explained in a way that puts the children at the centre, then it is not worth doing. I often suggest that schools do an audit of workload, or if that is not going to work in your setting, then do an individual audit of your own work patterns. Focus on the things that you need to do so that your pupils learn and make good progress, then identify the things you do that make little or no difference and stop putting pressure on yourself to get them done. For instance, if you spend hours on the internet looking for the perfect teaching clip or lesson plan to adapt for your pupils, you could save this time by devising one yourself, and while you plan it, you will have your own pupils in mind. We often fool ourselves that we are saving time, when we are not.

What is your most important function as a teacher – knowing what your children have learnt, and what your next steps are?

This should never mean endless spreadsheets of data, but rather the use of effective, formative assessments in the classroom in every lesson. As both teachers and leaders, your time is finite, so part of managing your workload is about protecting your time and putting boundaries in place.

Set boundaries and keep them

When I trained to be a head teacher, you were deemed to be effective if you had an 'open door' policy, and it was something that I was proud to share with my community, whether that was pupils, staff, parents or governors; however, in reality, that policy became one of the factors that led to my experience of chronic burnout. You must learn to protect yourself from taking on all the concerns that your community is carrying around with them, as you do not have all the answers. Of course, there is a fine balance to be found here – the longer I was in leadership, the more I was able to find that balance. My door was always open to the children in my school; I encouraged them to see my room as a safe space and was ready to take in dysregulated, vulnerable children at any time of day, despite who I was meeting with – the adults could always wait, but children could not. It is interesting that some staff found this difficult and would try to dissuade children from coming in, but did not show the same resistance to a parent with a minor concern that could have been dealt with by someone other than the head teacher.

An open door policy for a small number of staff can mean that they will come to your door at every opportunity to get you to solve a problem that they perceive they have. Even in a small school, this means that you could be having these types of conversations with people for most of the day – and we wonder why we never get things ticked off our 'to do' lists. Being a sounding board for your staff is necessary at times, but not *all* the time. Try to use some coaching methods in these instances, ask them to reframe the issue or try to think of at one least one way through the difficulty themselves, before sitting down with them to find solutions. When people stop you in the corridor or knock on your door with that question, 'have you got five minutes?' – take a breath and think; you may genuinely have time there and then to talk, but firstly consider if these conversations ever are just five minutes, and secondly judge whether you would be better off scheduling those conversations for later in the day. We know that it is human nature to want immediate answers when something has upset us and made us angry, and often, once we have had time to pause and reflect, a solution often comes to us more easily. For the community to thrive, everyone should have some autonomy; they should know that they are trusted to make decisions but also know that their leaders will support them when they need it.

Maintain a sensible perspective

As educational professionals, we have taken on this role because we know we can make a difference to people's lives, and we take this very seriously – but sometimes we may lose all perspective of what we can realistically achieve as one individual and how well we can perform our role. Perfectionism is something teachers need to let go of very quickly for them to be able to thrive in the job. Dr. Emma Kell talks about this in her 2024 TEDx Talk, and the book I referred to earlier, Teacher Wellbeing and Self Care. Educational professionals would benefit from taking the lead from health and social care professionals to adapt the 'good enough' phrase that was coined by Donald Winnicott in the 1950s when referring to 'the good-enough mother'. Winnicott was a well-known psychoanalyst and pediatrician, who theorised that mothers who responded to their baby's every sound, and tried to be there *all* the time, burnt out, as they were trying too hard and were too scared to make mistakes. This idea of 'good enough' is now used widely in many professions, as it gives us the foundations to protect ourselves from doing too much.

Take a moment:

- **Next time you are feeling the pressure of producing something in a particular way, i.e. your end-of-term nativity or your presentation for governors, ask yourself – What will good enough look like? – and aim for that. (Afterall no one was expecting a West End production!)**

Prioritising

This is key to managing your workload, but the word itself sends shivers down my spine as it is something that I can struggle with. Since being diagnosed with ADHD, in April 2024, I now understand my brain much better and allow myself some slack for not being able to prioritise everything all the time. I am getting much better at it in the workplace, however I still have some way to go with my own domestic and personal admin. Teaching and leading are very busy, demanding jobs, and the need to prioritise is essential; we all know there are pressure points in the school year where this necessity increases. There are many apps out that are designed to make organising your work easier – I am yet to find one that works for me, but remember, I am not neuro-typical, and often have to devise my own strategies A tactic that does work is putting my phone on airplane mode, setting a timer for an hour and putting it out of reach – it amazes me how much I can get done in that hour without the distraction of constant phone notifications.

The joy of a 'what I have done' list

I have yet to meet a teacher who does not have a 'To-Do List' in some form or other, and these are great, but to make them more efficient, put the items on the list in order of importance and work according to priority. On a recent coaching call with an aspiring head teacher as part of their National Professional Qualification for Headship (NPQH) training, I shared something I do when I am feeling particularly overwhelmed, and this is writing a 'What I have done' list. A simple idea, shared with me by someone many years ago, that you may initially think is a waste of your time – it really isn't – because it makes clear what you have achieved and identifies where your time has been spent. Some people will take five minutes at the end of each day to do this or the end of each week – how you do it is up to you. Seeing that list written down will not only show you what you have done, but also reveal that many of these things were not on your initial 'To-Do List'; they were additional, critical tasks that needed your time and wisdom to solve. This ongoing re-prioritising of tasks is something we do all the time in our personal life; you may plan to do a food shop, walk the dog and clean the house, but if your elderly parents need you in an emergency, or one of your adult children wants to FaceTime for over an hour in preparation for an important job interview, you would prioritise these things and realise that a cleanish house and a shorter walk for the dog are good enough.

Tools for prioritising

The Eisenhower Matrix is something that many leaders use, and when I deliver training for Schools, Students and Teachers network (SSAT) on the implementation and embedding of Embedding formative assessment (EFA), it is a tool that is recommended. **Stephen Covey** in his book *The 7 Habits of Highly Effective People* talks about this matrix in detail, and this has increased its popularity with leaders. As you might have surmised, it was created by US President Dwight D. Eisenhower during his term in office in the 1950s. It is an effective tool used to organise and prioritise your activities and uses the following headings:

1. **Do**
2. **Schedule**
3. **Delegate**
4. **Delete**

The last bullet point is my favourite. Why? I think it is because being able to have the option of deleting a task identifies tasks that are key to progress, and those that would have been a nice, but non-urgent, added extra. There is no shame in thinking that what was initially a great idea turns into one that you no longer have the time or capacity to fit in right now.

Take a moment:

- **Try using a 'What I have done list' and note down how it made you feel – was it a more positive experience than finishing the week looking at another 'To Do List' that is only half finished? Remember perspective is everything.**

Looking after yourself

One of the many books that I read avidly during my recovery from burnout was *School Leaders Matter. Preventing Burnout, Managing Stress and Improving Well-being* by Helen Kelly (2023). Helen is now a writer, speaker and consultant in the field of well-being, but prior to this she had a successful career leading international schools. Reading the preface of her book made me weep, because her story is so like mine, except it happened in 2018–2019. After her stay in hospital with cardiac-related ill health, she was told that it was all down to stress and that she would have to look at her lifestyle and see where she could make changes to eradicate stress as far as possible.

This was her reaction: 'I felt like I have been punched in the stomach, and I burst into tears. I thought that they were going to fix me, but instead I was being told that I had to fix myself' (page xiii in Preface).

At the time of reading this, I could entirely relate to how she was feeling, and I still can.

I wonder how many readers of this book feel the same way. To me, it was like a voice from the dark telling me that I was not going mad, these things *had* really happened to me and reading her book helped me to decide what my next steps would be. During the aftermath of my burnout, I tried to apply for ill-health retirement but kept being told by the medical experts from the DFE/Teachers Pensions that the cardiac symptoms I had were not stress related, despite every medical expert who dealt with me personally saying the opposite. I did not get ill-health retirement and am patiently waiting for my 55th birthday to come round. Like Helen, I did not return to headship but have created a new path in the world of education that is more suited to my health at this time in my life. However, what if all leaders were put in this position? There would not be enough head teachers to lead our schools – a situation that we are not that far from.

How does sleep help?

Helen's book is full of strategies for a range of stakeholders, including government, to support the well-being of school leaders and to protect them from the situation that we both found ourselves in. I have spoken to Helen through the power of social media, and as well as her book, she has created some excellent resources for school leaders. One of these is 'Sleep Well, Lead Well. A Guide to Improving Sleep for Leaders' and can be found at www.drhelenkelly.com.

We imagine that it is a given that we all know the importance of getting a good night's sleep, but do we really believe it? It is not hard to find information about the necessity of good sleep, yet as busy professionals we ignore it – and at our peril. So many important things happen to our body and our brain when we sleep, that any disruption to that can have serious consequences for our health. When we sleep, the cells in our body repair themselves, our energy levels are topped up, and important hormones and proteins are released into our bloodstream. In our brains, at different stages of our rapid eye movement (REM) and non-REM sleep cycles, we can flush out toxins and waste, consolidate our memories and even strengthen the connections of our neurons. If these things don't happen, and if we regularly have less than seven hours' sleep a night, then we are 50% more likely to be at risk of heart disease, stroke and depression. As I write this, I am thinking about my own sleep habits and comparing them to when I was a serving head teacher. The habits that I have now would probably still be deemed not as effective as they could be if I was to discuss them with my general practitioner (GP), but I have made some significant improvements. However, I admit that I still sleep with my phone next to my bed (for emergencies, as we have elderly parents) and I don't always stick to a regular routine as the alarm will get snoozed at the weekend. Anyone who knows me will tell you about my love of an afternoon nap; despite medication for ADHD, this is still quite a regular occurrence, and it never fails to astonish me how comfortable my bed is at 3 pm in the afternoon rather than at 3 am in the morning. However, I no longer drink wine every night to ensure I can sleep, and I don't have to ask my GP for sleeping tablets to help when things are really stressful. I can stop working in front of a screen with hours to spare, and night-time baths and podcasts are no longer a luxury, but something I always have time for if I want to. As a head teacher, I would spend most nights during the week unable to sleep, ruminating on events or planning things that I needed to do; most weekends I would fall asleep on the sofa during the day. Looking back, it is very clear how unhealthy that was for me, but at the time it had become the norm. I highly recommend that you download Helen's guide to sleep, as it is an excellent resource, and her advice about practicing self-compassion, and strategies to manage and reduce rumination are useful.

Picking your battles

'Pick your battles' is a phrase you will hear me use a lot in both professional and personal situations. However, I will admit that it is not advice I have always been prepared to take myself – particularly in my early headship and when parenting teenage girls. I will admit that I made many mistakes, but after a while I began to begrudgingly learn from them. Two important things helped me with this: one was the incredible training from Chimp Management (Peters, 2012), and the other was realising that I cared too much about other people's perception of me, when I shouldn't have done; instead of being brave enough to deal with demanding situations in the way that I wanted to, I was dealing with them in a way that I thought other people expected me to.

Do not be who other people want you to be

Just like Jacinda Aherne, I have been accused many times of being too soft, too kind and too empathetic. I was told that as a head teacher, children should fear me, and that I needed to raise my voice and use punitive measures to instill discipline and respect from them. I always found it astonishing that so many people were generous with their opinions about how I should lead a school, when they had no experience of doing so themselves. As a new head, I wanted to apply what I had practiced in previous roles about relationships, to cultivate a sense of belonging and trust to a school community instead of fear and flexibility rather than a regime of non-negotiables, but I will admit at times I found myself falling into the trap of behaving how other people thought I should. Did their methods work for me? Absolutely not.

Do not let other people's attitudes to leadership diminish the light that comes from your values, because they should drive everything you do.

This is not easy at all, as we are never the finished article. As humans, we naturally turn to others for guidance and reassurance, and we want them to be proud of what we do. However, if it feels wrong to you, then it *is* wrong, and having integrity is far more important than trying to have people in your corner whose values do not align with yours – as leaders, we often learn this the hard way. Values are discussed in greater depth in Chapter 4.

Dealing with challenging situations and emotions

Whether you are dealing with a dysregulated child, a member of staff or a parent, it is easy to lose sight of what the most important thing is, and instead fall into the trap of wanting to 'win the argument' and show everyone that you are in charge; this is ineffective leadership and will no doubt impact negatively on the well-being of all parties involved.

At this point, I want to refer to Dr. Peters and his Chimp Paradox model. Remember that in his model there are two key elements that I want to expand on, the idea that the frontal lobe is the human part of the psychological brain and the limbic is the chimp. The premise is that we all have a human and a chimp in our psychological brain, and they are two separate entities, with their own responses and reactions to events. You can see how this links to the idea that we resort to our basic primal instincts when in danger – that is where our chimp is necessary – in many ways our chimp keeps us safe. The issue with the human and the chimp is that they think and react differently to the same situation; the human will try to think logically about things and deal with the facts as they see them, whereas the chimp deals with emotions and will try to overpower the human with an emotional response. This model is a brilliant way of explaining our emotional reactions to situations to young people, and there are various children's books that have been published by the Chimp Paradox business to use with younger children.

As school leaders or teachers in the classroom, it is important that we stay in 'human mode' during any challenging encounter. Any encounter between two people when they are both in Chimp mode will be a disaster in terms of resolving a problem and finding solutions. I alluded earlier to the fact that we often forget what is important during these situations – what is the *most important* thing in nearly all difficult conversations?

The key thing we want to end up with is an outcome all parties are at least satisfied with, that everyone feels they have been listened to, and any dysregulation (in adults or children) has been de-escalated.

If a child shouts at you, is your aim to shout louder? If a parent swears at you, is it your aim to swear back with a more offensive word? (not if you want to keep your job). If a member of staff complains about a situation, is it your aim to complain about them in return? Of course not, but too often we see these things as a power battle where someone must come out of the scenario victorious, and someone is defeated. For many years, a colleague would advise me in the following ways – 'you need to do this' or 'you must say this' – whenever I found myself with a problem to unpick. I am sure that these suggestions were meant to be helpful, but just take a moment to really look at the language they were using. These pearls of wisdom only ever considered the perspective of the school, and never the other party; they assumed that to act like an assertive leader, I needed to win every argument and not take into consideration what a satisfactory outcome for *all* parties could look like.

Throughout my career, there have been so many examples of instances where a more satisfactory outcome would have been achievable if people had just kept calm and dealt with the initial situation with compassion, a change in their perception and a non-judgemental stance. Early in my headship, I was on the receiving end of a complaint from a parent that went as far as Ofsted and a governor panel, when it could have been dealt with effectively and quickly at the first mention of the issue. The original complaint was that the parent did not want their child to be sat where they were in class and asked for them to be moved. We managed to get so far down the road of the school's complaints procedure because right at the beginning there was a fundamental lack of understanding about what a satisfactory outcome would be – what would be good enough for all parties? Neither the teacher nor the parent could agree on an outcome as neither one of them wanted to be perceived to give in to the other. Both adults were unhappy with the situation they found themselves in, and so from this first exchange, there grew a long list of minor grievances from both parties that became major because of their individual perceptions of the situation. I can categorically say that in most interactions after that, both adults let their 'chimps' take over whenever they had to speak to each other. If my advice had been asked for initially, I would have simply moved the child – that was not a battle that I was prepared to fight, and as it turned out I was the one left to deal with a process that was a waste of both my time and my leadership skills.

When engaging in battle be prepared

In the past 12 years of headship, there have been battles that were worth fighting, and I have happily donned my battle gear and led the charge – but these battles were about having integrity and passion and putting the education of pupils *first*, and not the wounded pride of a teacher who was having a bad day. Of course, there will be some of you reading this thinking that I didn't show that member of staff much compassion, but in fact I did at the time, and it was probably misdirected; I should have been more honest with my evaluation of the situation at the time. As humans we make mistakes, but we must be honest about these mistakes and reflect on how we could have done things differently. I could have asked the pertinent question at the time: 'what is important here?'. Is it that one of the adults feels they have won, or that the pupil is comfortable and confident joining in with the learning because they are happy where they sit?

Using soft skills in hard situations

Another colleague who worked with me for many years would tell me that she envied my ability to talk to parents/staff who were angry or upset, and be able to get them to a place where we could agree a solution that suited everyone (of course, this is not always possible). I now realise that this is quite ironic, as in these situations, I engaged in the same strategies that I used when other people told me that I should be stricter and less approachable – so you can't please everyone, and nor should you try to. What model or template did I follow in these situations? If you had asked me 15 years ago, I don't know that I would have been able to articulate specific strategies that I employed – I would have put it down to be just being 'good with people', but this isn't true, as there have been many people I know who would argue that I was not particularly 'good' with them – that old devil called perception again! Now I am a lot older and maybe a little bit wiser; I can articulate some of the things that I have found to work for me. Firstly, If I know that I have a meeting scheduled that is going to be uncomfortable and will need me to be kind, but honest, then I will always plan for it. Dr. Peters calls this 'Chimp Proofing', and this is a term my husband and I still use regularly in a work context. I would think about what an ideal outcome would be and work backwards from there, then I would share this with appropriate people before the meeting. The Chimp Paradox refers to a model called 'The Square of Communication', which basically has the right person in the centre, and at the four corners there are right time, right place, right agenda and right way. Chapter 9 of the book *The Chimp Paradox*, 'The Planet Connect', is all about communicating effectively, and I highly recommend that you take a look at it.

> The key to communicating well is to prepare yourself.
>
> (Peters, 2012, p. 163)

In a professional situation I always try to be the human in the room, as a room full of chimps will never agree or consider compromising.

Let me give you an example.

Consider this scenario and think about 'The Square of Communication':

You have a situation where for several reasons a teacher on your staff has been not behaving according to the school expectations and in fact is not adhering to the teachers' standards in terms of professionalism. You have had two informal meetings with her to address issues, and despite agreements being made, several members of staff have reported to you that things have only got worse not better. In response to this, you have sent her an email, according to your policy regarding a more formal meeting at a designated time and date. The email was scheduled to send at 8:15 am, and at 8:30 am you are in a briefing with your business manager when the teacher, obviously upset, opens door to your office and demands to talk to you immediately. You ask her to come in and ask your business manager to leave. The teacher then begins to shout and be defensive about her behaviour and accusatory of yours and even uses the words 'bullying' and 'discrimination'. When she has finished, she leaves the office in tears and goes home.

It is clear that this is not an appropriate way to manage this, but what would have been more effective?

Events like this will happen when you are in a leadership position, and hindsight is always a wonderful thing – but the most important thing to remember is that you had a designated time and date arranged, and this would have been at least some way to be fulfilling the criteria of right time, right place, right people, right way. Your teacher had let her *chimp* take over and reacted emotionally and aggressively, and it would have been very hard for you not to react in the same way. Allowing her to hijack your meeting has left you in a position where she has made her own emotional state more heightened, she has accused you of certain behaviours, and as you let your business manager leave, you have no witnesses to any of this. In this incident, it would have been more appropriate to tell the upset teacher that she could not see you and she needed to attend the arranged meeting. If she had then acted inappropriately in front of other members of staff, this could be documented and used as more evidence regarding misconduct.

Strategies that can be used in unforeseen situations

If the situation is not scheduled, like many things in life, then I have a few strategies that come into play that work for me (after many years of practice, mistakes and reflection).

Imagine an irate parent in your reception area, making their annoyance obvious to anyone in the vicinity – we have all been there. My first strategy is to always smile, address them directly ('Hello Mr. X'), name their feelings (in the same way that you would a dysregulated child) 'I can see that you feel very strongly about this' and invite them into my office to discuss things further. This action of cutting them off politely and physically moving them will often change the dynamic of the interaction. Once in your office, the situation changes again, as this is where you feel comfortable – ask a member of staff to join you if you need to. I have had to work very hard to be able to act in a calm and professional manner on many occasions and remember that is exactly what we are all doing – acting. As a leader, there are many situations where you will feel threatened and you might be fighting hard not to go in to flight, fight or freeze, but I always tell myself I can do any of these afterwards if necessary. Keep smiling and ask the parent to explain to you calmly, as their manner could be seen as confrontational, exactly what they perceive to be the problem. The word 'perceive' is key, as we will all have differing perspectives of the same situation. Whatever you do, make sure that you listen (Manley Hopkinson would go as far as saying 'shut up and listen'), do not be too keen to answer straight away or justify what you think the situation really is. The next step is to repeat back to them what they have told you in your words (this is one I will always remember) –

> okay Mr. X you are upset about a playground incident that your child has told you about and you would like me to exclude a 4 year old child for poking their tongue out at your daughter – is this a correct summary?

Often, when you simplify things to this level, adults who have had the opportunity to calm down and feel listened to will realise that their feelings are not as valid as they might have first thought. Actually, in this situation, because I had taken time to get to know the family, I could see that in front of me I had a dad who had not had the best experiences at school himself, struggling to let go of his little girl, who had been in school only a matter of weeks and had no preschool experience. Subconsciously, Dad had been waiting for something to go wrong at school so he could justify his feelings of loss, remove his daughter and keep her at home, where he believed her to be safe. This child went on to remain at school through to year 6 and thrived, as her parents had more children and they found the process of them starting school easier; with time and patience, we were able to communicate positively about any further bumps in the road. If I had allowed my chimp to take over during that interaction, I firmly believe that the child would not have stayed with us and enjoyed all the experiences the school had to offer.

What did I do in my interaction with that parent? I listened, and for a short moment, I imagined what it was like to be him and to feel what he was feeling. Of course, there were onlookers in the office that day that I imagine thought that I should have dealt with things differently and shamed that dad for his actions. We shouldn't do this to adults any more than we should to children.

When having a courageous conversation, these are few things to remember:

- **Try to use 'gentle' non-emotional words.**
- **Always give the other person a chance to talk first and make sure you really listen.**
- **Be willing to see someone else's perspective and learn from this.**
- **Remember that opinions and emotions are not facts.**
- **Try to reason and discuss without confrontation.**
- **Compromise so that an outcome that satisfies everyone is reached.**
- **Stay outwardly calm.**

Take a moment:

- Can you think of a time where you wish you had reacted differently to a difficult situation? What would you change?
- Can you think of a time when you felt that someone should have reacted differently to you, and ultimately you felt unheard? What did you do about this?

Bibliography

Bethune, A. & Kell, E. (2020) *Teacher Wellbeing and Self Care – A Little Guide for Teachers.* Sage Publications.
Covey, S. (1989) *The 7 Habits of Highly Effective People.* Simon & Schuster.
Hopkinson, M. (2022) *Compassionate Leadership.* Little Brown.

Kelly, H. (2023) *School Leaders Matter: Preventing Burnout, Managing Stress and Improving Wellbeing.* Routledge, A Speechmark Book.

Nagoski, E. & Nagoski, A. (2019) *Burnout: The Secret to Solving the Sress Cycle.* Vermilion.

Peters, S. Dr. (2012) *The Chimp Paradox: The Science of Mind Managment for Confidence, Success, and Happiness.* Vermilion.

Puri, N. Dr. (2024) *What Are the Benefits of Hugging?* The Teacher Wellbeing Index.

Winnicott, D. (1962) *The Child and Family: First Relationships.* London Tavistock.

Values, ethos and culture – how to grow, sustain and nurture them

This chapter will explore the ideas that

- Creating a positive school culture is one of the hardest things to do well, but ultimately the most important.
- Your leadership values should align with your school values.
- The idea of belonging is key to a school culture that works.

There are many excellent books that have been written on these elements of leadership that look at them in more depth than I can here, but be under no illusion that the culture of a school is the key component for everyone in that community and beyond. A leader needs to create a healthy and authentic culture, and never one based on fear and recrimination – and this will take years to do successfully.

One thing I know is that schools run on human connections and the importance of *belonging* **not just 'fitting in'.**

We cannot force humans to fit into a box that is the wrong shape or size for them, yet so many schools continue with this 'one-size-fits-all' approach, everyone must dress the same, behave the same and learn the same. The reality of this approach is that it will never work for all people (big or small), and if that is the way you want your school to be, then please do not use the term 'inclusive' when you talk about your values.

Values

Take a moment:

- Look at the chart and choose six values that you think are the most important ones to you (don't try to distinguish between professional and personal, as in our work these will generally be the same).

Fairness	Mercy	Generosity	Resourcefulness	Open-mindedness
Trust	Happiness	Independence	Simplicity	Authenticity
Growth	Autonomy	Reliability	Creativity	Playfulness
Safety	Respect	Integrity	Duty	Courtesy
Dignity	Liberty	Love	Curiosity	Insight
Adventure	Equity	Belonging	Justice	Loyalty
Success	Excellence	Honesty	Order	Forgiveness
Kindness	Self-knowledge	Empathy	Understanding	Patience
Humour	Risk	Stability	Supportiveness	Self-control
Public Services	Inclusion	Compassion	Openness	Credibility
Humility	Nurture	Candour	Determination	Something else that you would put in?

Why values are important

This is an exercise widely used in coaching sessions (this table was shared with me by Dr. Emma Kell with her permission), and there are no right or wrong choices; the important part is recognising what it is you stand for. What are the things that define you and your beliefs? When you have aligned yourself with these, the problem that often arises is that you might begin to question whether your values are synchronised with those of your school – are you working somewhere where you feel you belong? If you are a leader starting on this journey of creating a positive, compassionate culture, how do you ensure that your values are central to it? Once you have defined your values, you might immediately recognise that they align with the values of your school and that is why you are there and thriving – I do hope this is the case.

In the past (and I suspect this is still happening in some establishments), the values of a setting would have been generated in a range of ways – maybe in a whole school session, or by leaders and governors only, or just by people at the top of your Trust (if you are in a large Academy Trust), or maybe they have been there for so long that no one remembers where they originated.

These are not values; they are just words.

They may be strategically placed on the walls and windows of your school and on all your communications, and no doubt they are important, but are they *really* the things that define you? These words (excellence, aspiration and respect) are used to influence your expectations of pupil behaviour and attitude, and will in turn support school improvement, but these won't work if you do not have the right values or moral principles behind them.

You will not find the values of a school on its walls – so where will you find them?

From my experience, you will see school values in several different ways and in several different places. You will see them in the way people speak *to* each other and *about* each other – this is so telling of whether a school has a positive or a toxic culture.

- How do all staff, including lunchtime staff, office staff and outside agencies, interact, talk to and about pupils and staff in the building?
- How does this play out in the staff room?
- Do people even use the staff room?
- How do the staff talk about the wider community as in parents and carers?
- Are they able to see someone else's perspective and have empathy for their position even if it is not the same as their own?

School values should be obvious in the policies and procedures that are in place also:

- What does their behaviour policy say – do all staff follow it?
- What does the marking policy say – does it recognise that written marking is not always necessary?
- Does the school encourage effective formative assessment strategies over coloured pens and targets?
- What does the policy around time off for staff look like?
- Can they watch their own children in important events?
- Can they attend funerals that are not just close family?
- Can they schedule appointments for their physical and mental health during the school day?

How do you feel when you walk around the school and go into classrooms?

- Do adults smile and welcome you in?
- Do the pupils jump up to talk about themselves and their learning?
- Are all children recognised as being part of the class, even if they sometimes need their space to regulate themselves?
- Can pupils tell you who their trusted adults are?

I could go on!

The link between values and a culture of compassion

A positive, compassionate culture relies on everyone having values that align and a moral compass that points generally in the same direction. There isn't a single document that can evidence this, not a school improvement plan, or a Special Educational Needs and Disabilities (SEND) code of practice or a staff handbook, but it is what the school shows you in its everyday practice. I have seen many documents in educational settings that say one thing, and what you see and hear in practice is the complete opposite.

How the community responds to a positive culture

During my research for this book, I have talked to school staff, governors, parents and children who have benefited from belonging in a community that shared a culture of compassion and kindness, and these are some of the things that they felt were important to them.

> The school had a strong, unified culture, where staff worked collaboratively, embodying shared values of respect, inclusivity, and care. This collective commitment provided an environment where children felt seen, valued and supported, creating a sense of belonging.
>
> Member of staff

> When I moved to this area with my children, I visited all the local schools with my eldest child who was 4. He chose this school, and when I asked him why, he said that the headteacher was so lovely and that she was talking to me and not just the adults. That simple act of connection stayed with us.
>
> Parent and child

> I truly believe that my son's experience at this school would have been vastly different without the compassionate leadership shown by the headteacher.
>
> Parent

> All staff were treated equally, and I think because of this, we were happy and fulfilled in our work. This had a ripple effect throughout the school, and because problems did not escalate, it enabled us all to work happily as a team.
>
> Member of support staff

> This school gave my three children the best start in life, which I believe contributed massively to them being the three fantastic adults they are today. No matter what their capabilities or personalities, they were understood, and this school will always have special memories in our hearts.
>
> Parent

A culture of kindness

Why is creating a culture of kindness and compassion important? Why do so many articles, books and research papers cite it as a key driver of effective leadership? As I said before, one of the reasons is that the teaching profession deals with humans on a day-to-day basis, and we all deserve to be treated with kindness and respect. **The VIA (Values in Action Inventory)** Insititute on Character identify kindness as a strength that sits within the virtue of *humanity*. They recognise that to be kind you need integrity and strong principles like honesty and compassion – the kind of values that you often see in people in caring professions.

The latest Teacher Wellbeing Index (2024) has the following statistics regarding the culture of schools and colleges:

- 50% of those surveyed said that the organisation's culture has a negative effect on the staff's mental health and well-being. This figure is actually a slight improvement on the 2023 results, which I find astounding. Just let this figure sink in for a moment.

- 38% of those surveyed said that the organisation did not support employees with mental health and well-being problems.

A Department for Education (DFE) report, 'The Working Lives of Teachers and Leaders' (2024) highlights the following:

- A significantly higher proportion of teachers and leaders consider their jobs impact more negatively on their personal life, and in fact, 73% claimed that they had no time for a personal life at all.

A culture of compassion means that you as a leader, or a member of staff, would be able to have challenging conversations, where you are giving or receiving feedback in a psychologically safe environment. Staff should know that feedback is not personal, that decisions are made based on what is right for the pupils and the wider school community. Courageous conversations are not about you or them as a person. In Dr. Stephen Peter's Chimp Paradox book, he refers to the fact that one in five people will not like you, and often for no justifiable reason. I know that sounds quite shocking, but there you have it – are you going to waste your time dwelling on that, or are you going to continue to make your leadership decisions based on positive values? As a leader you need to model that; so, whilst difficult conversations are just that, you will not shy away from them; instead you will conduct them in an honest and open way. I agree with Brene Brown when she advocates that avoiding these conversations is not kind; it is not kind to the person that you need to have the conversation with, and it is often not kind to the people who work in the same team as this person, as they are often the ones effected most directly. In a school situation, when a member of staff needs support, not dealing with this as a leader will almost certainly have a negative impact on the children. So, in this instance, it is important to go back to our 'WHY?' – which is that if the education of the children is negatively impacted, you are not being kind to them. Having these conversations and offering staff coaching from yourself or another professional is one of the most powerful things you can do for your whole school community.

A culture of compassion creates a safe space, a feeling of psychological safety for all its community. Some of the things that you will not hear is people talking about each other, rather than to each other, or leaders telling staff half-truths to appease them. It is not effective leadership to avoid difficult emotions, as this can often lead to confusion and a lack of clarity about the expectation of the school; leaders need to confront complex feelings with honesty, and that sometimes requires bravery.

The importance of trust

Trust is a key element in creating a culture of compassion, as this type of culture has positive relationships at the heart of it. If there is trust in an organisation, then employees and other members of that community are more willing to be vulnerable based on the knowledge that those around them are honest, open and benevolent. Naturally, an environment that feels safe psychologically takes time to create and embed, and very much depends on how much your team trust you as a leader.

It is common practice for incoming head teachers to want to make changes to their new school as soon as they can, and in many cases, they are necessary for the pupils and staff; however, often it is because the head teacher is simply keen to make their mark. My advice would always be (unless these changes are implemented because of a serious safeguarding issue) take all the time you need to talk to people (big and little) and to make your own judgements about what needs to happen first; after all, it was their school first before it was yours. Take a leaf from Manley's book and 'shut up and listen'.

If the culture is not how you want it, then building relationships based on trust is key – but this will not be a quick fix. A number of schools that I visit in my varying roles have had a string of head teachers, or executive leaders, over a short period of time that have made changes and then moved on, only to be replaced by another leader who repeats the same pattern. It is more important in these situations to spend time in discussion with the staff and school community, so that they can get the measure of you as a leader, and the values that are central to the culture you want to build.

Building trust from the beginning

There are many strategies you can employ during your early tenure that will encourage the roots of trust to start appearing in the community. A key one is to really try to make those members of the community that feel invisible, for whatever reason, feel visible – take time to talk to them, ask their opinions and thank them for what they do. With every action, try to model that you are thinking about others, and that you are listening, and if you can, start to think about them when planning the changes you want to make. When I coach clients who feel stuck in their role, or are unhappy with the culture of their workplace, I often ask if they have spoken to the relevant people about this; invariably, I will be told that they have, but they feel that they have not been listened to. Feeling unheard creates toxicity in any environment and is really damaging for the well-being of the people feeling that way. Of course, as a leader you cannot always make the changes that someone is asking for, but it is important to take the time to listen and return to them at some point with the reasoning behind your decisions – those people who have come to you will, at the very least, accept that you have listened and thought about a solution.

Being visible is key

The initial stages of building trust rely on you being a visible presence around the school. The wider school community, the parents, carers and guardians of the children in your care, will appreciate daily contact with you when you are at the school gate meeting and greeting. I recognise that this often coincides with important phone calls, and staff wanting '5 minutes of your time before the madness starts' but establishing a ritual of value for the wider community, which becomes a regular occurrence, shows them that they are important. It may not feel very strategic, but it goes back to the centrality of the relationships that you build and how they are needed to nurture the culture moving forward. During these moments, you have the ideal opportunity to talk with parents in an informal setting and ask how things are going, enabling you or your team to head off any issues before they grow into bigger problems. There is no doubt that some parents will look out for you every morning, with something important to discuss. My advice is to look for the less confident ones and engage with them – they will appreciate being listened to. Get to know everyone's names and their family situations as soon as you are able to, and ensure you address them by their names when you talk to them. Take a moment to interact with any younger children, remember little things they have told you and bring them up again – they will be amazed that you have remembered. Always be positive and always smile. I can imagine the thoughts of leaders reading this who work in large schools and communities, and I understand that this is not possible for you. However, you will have a larger team of leaders, so make sure they are doing this on your behalf. I can guarantee it will still be appreciated, and those parents and carers will begin to trust you and recognise that your intentions are good.

Being a presence around and about inside school is harder to get right as you don't want the staff to think that you are constantly watching and checking up on them. However, one thing that I learnt early on in headship is that people really appreciate you 'checking in' with them. Poking your head round the door of a classroom whilst teachers are setting up the day is a good indicator of how they are feeling. You will soon gauge whether they need more of your time or merely a quick how are you? and a thank you of some sort will be enough to start their day on a positive note. Do not underestimate the power of these small actions – being around means that if there is an undercurrent of unhappiness, you will feel it and be able to deal with it.

In addition, being a presence for the pupils is crucial – you cannot build relationships with children from your office, and particularly not with your most vulnerable pupils. You need to show an interest in them, talk to them and, importantly, make sure that when they need you to stay regulated and be there for them, you can do it. Please encourage your staff to send pupils to you for positive reasons, so that you can show them you are proud of their efforts, and if a child needs to be with you because they are struggling, go to them in situ and invite them to join you. You are not being weak; you are being kind, and you are building trust.

For the purposes of research for the book, I had the pleasure of interviewing school leaders from a range of different contexts; one of these was Sam Sillito who, by the time this book is published, will have left headship after 23 years in different schools and begun a new role within a local authority school improvement team, where she will be a huge asset. We talked in depth about the idea of a positive school culture and how it takes work, passion and clear communication with all stakeholders. Sam described how she leads her current school and says that 'Every day I am a presence around school; I am positive and upbeat and show a consistency of mood to everyone'.

She says her school culture is based on trust, and their recent focus has been on exploring self-efficacy with her community (self-efficacy is covered in Chapter 5). She prefers to use a coaching style of leadership and has invested a small amount of her overall school budget to use an independent coach as personalised staff development for members of her team with positive impact. She has led schools through different changes over her 23 years, including closing a school and opening a new one, which was an amalgamation of two existing schools and the tragic death of a pupil. Her leadership experience is vast.

Sam uses the theories of 'the transition curve' and 'transactional analysis' with her team on a regular basis and finds them incredibly useful when explaining the process of change within the organisation. The transition curve began with the work of Elizabeth Kubler Ross in the 1960s, and it was used as a tool for recognising and supporting the emotional reactions that come with grief. It was known then as the *change curve*. During the 1990s, this became a tool that was used in businesses and was later named the *transitional curve*. It was made popular in 2000 by psychologist John Fisher, and his Personal Transition Curve is now used extensively in counseling and business coaching. Transitional analysis is a psychoanalytic theory which is used to understand the different emotional states people might be in when communicating with others. In leadership, the use of this particular theory is helpful to understand and change behaviours, improve communication and promote self-awareness. This links us back to Daniel Goleman and his work on empathy and highlights that leading people is a complex and multifaceted occupation.

In the same way that Dr. Peters advises that we plan for courageous conversations, Sam has adopted her own style of planning for these with a football analogy.

> Before any meeting that I know could be challenging I always think about the outcome that we need and I draw that as a football goal, I then draw some balls and in them write out the steps that I am going to need to take, I then have what I call my red herrings in the shape of defenders and I think about what people in the meeting might say to stop us scoring that goal.

The method you use is a matter of personal choice, but it seems that good practice is to always know what you will settle for at the end of a meeting, bearing in mind that compromise nearly always comes into play (and so it should).

Regarding trust, Sam and I both talked passionately about why this is so important and how you can encourage your community to trust you and begin to believe in what you stand for. Sam talked about the need to prove yourself time and time again, and that is where your daily contact with people is vital. That contact needs to be positive, celebrating successes, however small, as it shows you are noticing when people are doing good things. One of Sam's clear pieces of advice is to 'say it like it is!'. She advocates that you 'should be honest about the challenges that the school is facing, the issues that need to be addressed and make it obvious what you will and won't accept'.

Sam uses a similar strategy to Paul Dix in his book *When the Adults Change, Everything Changes: Seismic Shifts in School Behaviour* (2017), who advocates to use with children regarding behaviour, and that is to praise in *public,* and to engage in conversations about changing practice in *private*. Sam and I agreed that being honest is something that comes with time and experience as it is often human nature to water down your message to stop feelings being hurt. But as Brene Brown would say, this is not *kind* leadership.

How do school staff feel about a culture of compassion?

In conversation with a range of non-leadership school staff, I asked what they wanted to see in their leaders and how they could develop a positive culture; these are some of the things that were discussed.

One teacher with many years of experience said that leadership needs to start from a place of trust.

> Leaders should notice the little things that you do and acknowledge them personally.

Many staff have reiterated this and said that the personal touch is always more appreciated than a generic thank you email at the end of a challenging week, month or term. That generic email is necessary in large establishments, but somewhere along the line staff need to be told *in person* that they are doing well, and that their efforts have been noticed.

In terms of values, the same teacher said that in his experience people respect leaders who are brave enough to challenge the behaviour of any member of the community that goes against the values of the school. For example, if you are promoting your school as inclusive, make sure that anyone who uses language that belittles or underestimates a child's ability to learn should not be used by staff anywhere in the school or beyond the gate.

School staff also commented on the feeling of being valued and being listened to as key qualities that support their well-being. Despite my admission that my 'open door' policy became unsustainable, it was a common aspect that staff appreciated. So this has to be about getting the balance right and ensuring staff understand why sometimes the door has to be shut, but with strategies in place to support this – like taking your concerns to another member of Senior Leadership Team (SLT) in that moment or putting it in an email to use as an agenda item for a meeting at a more appropriate time.

Actions will always be noticed

As school leaders, one thing to remember is that if you say you are going to do something, then make sure you do it – sounds so simple. This can be a small action like passing on a message or something more important like attending or arranging a follow-up meeting. If, like me, you know that you will forget some things, then have a strategy for this. If a parent ever tried to give me a message for the office whilst I was on the gate, I would make a joke out of it and send them in to the office themselves; parents soon realised that despite my best intentions, I wouldn't always remember that their child needed a school dinner. However, if it was something more important I had agreed to, then I would make sure it was done, or at least passed on to the most relevant member of staff to take action – these things are noticed. I ensure I ask people to hold me to account; on many occasions, I would ask the office staff to remind me that something needed doing so that I could be sure that I would get done (this is something I have learnt that my attention-deficit/hyperactivity disorder (ADHD) brain needs).

I cannot stress enough how important trust is to being a compassionate leader, but trust, like kindness, doesn't mean accommodating everyone else's opinions and demands. If you have to have difficult conversations (and you will, sometimes daily), then reminding people of the school values and expectations and not presenting them with the solution that they wanted can be done in a way that is kind and honest and in a manner which maintains your integrity. The results of this will be people acknowledging your integrity and accepting that you will stand by the decision that you make; whether they agree with your choices or not, they will know that you have listened to their perspective and taken that into account.

Kindness is a language which the deaf can hear and the blind can see.

Mark Twain

A culture of belonging

Dr. Steve Peters in *The Chimp Paradox* discusses that the chimp has an instinctive need to be a part of a troop, and I believe this to be true of the human part our psychological brain too. Our troop or tribe, or whatever you would like to call them, are the people that we rely on to support us. In most cases, we have a professional troop and a personal one. In a school context, this creates the sense of belonging, but it is important that you recognise who are the right people to have in your troop and are not – for me this would depend on us sharing *values* but not necessarily backgrounds and experiences. How you recognise these people is not always straightforward, and it can be even more complex to reach a position where they start to buy in to your values or find a different place to work that fits with their values. However, this is where those courageous and kind conversation come into play again.

> Take a moment:
> Who is in your professional troop?

- **Are there colleagues that you gravitate towards at meetings?**
- **Do you have a WhatsApp group of other leaders so that you can discuss local issues?**
- **Which of your governors would you share your honest concerns with about your budget or staffing?**
- **Would you count your school improvement partner as someone to be trusted and part of your troop?**

Over the decades that I have worked in the education sector, I have been sold many myths, as I am sure you have too. One from the early days was *don't smile until Christmas.* This little gem was given to student teachers in the 1990s as a behaviour management strategy for your first term in teaching. The second one I heard repeatedly when I secured my headship was to remember that *I was not in that role to make friends and that I did not need to be liked.* Both educational myths are so far off the mark when it comes to compassionate leadership, as relationships are at the very heart of creating a successful culture. Of course, your entire purpose as a school leader is not about making friends, but it is about forging good relationships that foster an environment of care and kindness towards the whole community.

> To me, a leader is only as good as the relationships that they foster, and the word relationship is more profound than leadership.
>
> Hopkinson (2022)

Simon Sinek talks about getting the culture right in the workplace and encouraging a sense of belonging in his book *Leaders Eat Last: Why Some Teams Pull Together* and Others Don't (2019). Simon talks about our need to feel safe in our workplace, and this feeling of psychological and physical safety will lead to a feeling of belonging, which in turn leads to staff being more innovative as they know that they are trusted to try new things and make mistakes in the process. Are we not always telling our pupils it is okay to make mistakes, as that is how we learn? It should not be any different for adults in school. Now I know that as school leaders we get very little time to read as much as we would like, especially when it comes to reading for our professional development – but if nothing else, try to read and make notes on Chapters 17 and 18 of *Leaders Eat Last* (Sinek, 2019) as they focus on the importance of a positive culture and how to create one. Chapter 18 has the subtitle of 'I Before You. Me Before We'. You may be nodding your head right now thinking about someone who has been a part of your troop/tribe that worked in exactly that way – don't let that person be *you*. A sense of belonging comes through having a 'Circle of Safety' according to Sinek, and if you don't have this as a leader, then it is something that you need to develop as a matter of urgency.

> Inside a Circle of Safety, when people trust and share their successes and failures, what they know and what they don't know, the result is innovation. It's just natural.
>
> (Leaders Eat Last, p. 170)

In my experience, if you create a 'Circle of Safety' in your school, whether that is your senior leadership team or a teaching and learning community, then what develops is a place where you hear and participate in rich and useful professional dialogue. This valuable dialogue drills down to the central purpose of the role of educators – and that is to improve standards for the pupils in your care. Conversations concentrate on pedagogy and evidence-based reading creating an environment where staff are able to talk about what they have been working on in their classrooms, and sharing their successes, and being honest about practices that didn't work so well, with no judgement attached. This culture of compassion fosters a culture of innovative practises and collaboration, with a common focus on getting it right for the community. Surely, this is what we want for our schools?

Integrity

Integrity is a value that is also key to any school setting or workplace creating the right culture to thrive in – but what does it mean?

The *Oxford Dictionary* defines integrity as the 'quality of being honest and having strong moral principles'. The *Merriam–Websters Collegiate Dictionary* defines integrity as 'the adherence to a code of especially moral or artistic values'. If you want to show integrity in a workplace as a leader, then ensuring that you follow a set of rules or moral principles, even when no one is looking, is really what it is all about. It involves taking responsibility for your actions, showing respect for the team and maintaining a positive attitude. This is particularly important when leading a school, as you are setting the direction and the vision of the entire establishment, and the other members of your community need to trust that you are doing this for the right reasons. If your staff do trust you, then the likelihood is that they will follow you and be supportive of the improvements that need to be made. However, you must continue to communicate with them honestly about how things are progressing and advise them if there needs to be a change of direction. Keeping colleagues part of the process, so they remain invested in the outcome, ensures staff are not merely being compliant – Manley Hopkinson refers to this as 'commitment vs compliance' (2022).

During my discussion with Sam Sillito regarding culture, I asked her how *belonging* was important to her and what it looked like in her setting. Sam talked about belonging coming from a feeling of 'sharedness' (we weren't sure if it was a word, but we liked it!) and everyone on the staff feeling valued. She has worked hard to build her staff so that there is always enough cover, using their own higher-level teaching assistants to teach when other staff need time off. Sam's own view on leave is much the same as mine and many others when it comes to leading with compassion.

She says, 'everyone has those moments in life when they need to else where and when that happens, the team will step in'.

> What goes around comes around. Treat people with respect and kindness and they will generally do the same.
>
> Sam Sillito

The Teacher Wellbeing Index 2024 reports that these are the things that respondents identified as factors in building a 'good culture'.

- Good leadership.
- Good staff relationships.
- Staff feel supported.
- Staff experience good levels of trust and autonomy.
- Staff feel appreciated.
- Good staff and pupil relationships.
- The school/college makes a meaningful difference to pupils.
- The school/college lives its values.
- Staff have a good work-life balance.
- Good line management procedures.
- Good pupil behaviour.

Each and every one of these points needs to be unpicked to find the core of what makes them good, but it is an excellent place to start.

Sinek has this to say regarding his work with businesses and chief executive officers (CEOs): 'Customers will never love a company until the employees love it first' (2019). I firmly believe that we can apply this theory directly to educational settings and translate it to this little gem of wisdom.

Pupils/parents will never love a school until the members of staff love it first. Take a moment:

- Spend some time around the school picking up clues about your culture – is it what you think it is?
- Refer to the questions asked earlier in the chapter about where you can identify the culture of your setting.
- Ask your governors, SLT and pupils to do their analysis and report back.

Bibliography

Brown, B. (2018) *Dare to Lead: Brave Work, Tough Conversations, Whole Hearts*. Vermillion.

DFE (2024) The Working Lives of Teachers and Leaders. Wave 1 Core Report Ref: ISBN 978-1-83870-447-6, RR1321.

Dix, P. (2017) *When the Adult Change, Everything Changes, Seismic Shifts in School Behaviour*. Independent Thinking Press.

Hopkinson, M. (2022) *Compassionate Leadership*. Little Brown.

Peters, S. P. Dr. (2015) *The Chimp Paradox: The Science of Mind Management for Confidence, Success and Happiness*. Penguin Random House.

Sinek, S. (2019) *Leaders Eat Last: Why Some Teams Pull Together and Others Don't*. Penguin Random House.

Teacher Wellbeing Index 2024.

Viacharacter.org Values in Action Inventory.

# Compassion, coaching and self-efficacy – professional development for the whole team

This chapter will explore the ideas that

- Compassion should start with you.
- Coaching is a highly effective way to develop your staff.
- Self-efficacy is key to a positive culture.
- Self-efficacy can be grown through coaching.

Put yourself first (sometimes)

For much of this book, the focus has been on how to act compassionately towards others. However, one key point that should be remembered always is that compassion must start with *us* – this goes back to the idea of 'good enough' and that we cannot be all things to all people all of the time. To avoid compassion fatigue and ultimately, burnout, we must remember what we need and what nourishes us. We read this advice in numerous books, research papers, magazines, blogs and websites, yet we still find it hard (some would say impossible) to do. We have all heard the quote, 'In case of an emergency, put on your own oxygen mask first.' and others such as 'You can't pour from an empty cup.' (although I always wonder why you would want to pour from a cup and not a jug.). These idiomatic expressions tell us the same thing, and they are sound reminders to ourselves that we cannot help and support others if we are too tired or unwell because we have not looked after ourselves. However, to really do this, many of us (and I know I did) will have to work on our own beliefs and reframe how we feel about taking time for ourselves. For me this came about through coaching, but you can do this for yourself if you take the time to really try. I totally agree with what head teacher Sam Sillito had to say about being present in school and showing a consistent mood to keep everyone else level and calm but beware of interpreting this as a necessity to ignore your own emotions as a leader – on the contrary, having an awareness of your emotions and acknowledging them is vital.

So how do we show our community our outwardly facing emotions, yet acknowledge our more negative inner emotions, understand them and ultimately not allow them to take over?

Who do you turn to?

In some cases, this is where Sinek's 'Circle of Safety' would come in very handy, if you are lucky enough to have one. During my discussions with Sam, she talked about where she goes when she needs to have, for want of a better expression, 'a big old rant!'.

Whilst I'm sure that this is relatable for many when something specific has upset us, what I really want to explore here is why we need to be kinder and more compassionate to ourselves when self-generated anxiety threatens to overwhelm – because the majority of us have the natural tendency to think about ourselves and our self-worth in a critical and negative manner, and this can add fuel to the smouldering fire of burnout.

As someone who has lived for over half a century, I have met many people in my lifetime and not all of them have been hard on themselves. I have met my fair share of people who project an image of confidence and self-assuredness that I have envied. Naturally, I have also met people who project an image of arrogance and ignorance, and when interacting with them, it is not usually envy that is my overriding emotion. It would not be healthy for us all to think about ourselves in that way (or infact true), but we should be able to talk to ourselves and about ourselves in a way that is not damning or disparaging.

How do you describe yourself?

How we think about ourselves is important – when coaching I often ask clients if they would talk to their best friend, partner or children the way they talk to themselves in their heads. The answer will always be no – so why is it okay to do it to ourselves?

Helen Russell has written a wonderful book that discusses the fact that many of us have this constant negative commentary in our brains. The book *How to Be Sad: Everything I've Learned about Getting Happier, by Being Sad, Better* (2021) is well worth delving into – it was one I enjoyed listening to whilst driving or doing jobs around the house, although I did have to keep stopping what I was doing (not the driving) to write notes, as it is full of helpful and relatable information.

The importance of words

One of the things discussed in this book is that words can change your life, and the way you speak to yourself is crucial – as I alluded to earlier, this is where coaching can come in if you find you cannot change this narrative for yourself. One pivotal idea is that we need to change the way we talk to ourselves; we all have an internal monologue (if you are attention-deficit/hyperactivity disorder (ADHD) like me, then it would be a dream to have just the one voice in my head) and that internal monologue is never very positive about ourselves. There is research that highlights how many thoughts you have in a day – some schools of thought say it is between 60,000 and 80,000, whilst others cite a much higher number – often these thoughts are either about the past or worrying about the future, and can lead to a spiralling of negative feelings directed inwards at ourselves. In my leadership role, I was always telling myself, in the run up to a big event, that I was not clever enough or knowledgeable enough to do it well, and after an event, I would always be asking why I forgot to say X or telling me that I could have done it better by doing Y.

It can be incredibly hard to remove ourselves from this constant stream of negative feedback, yet in her book Russell talks about one strategy that has stuck with me, and I pass it on at every opportunity; she refers to this internal voice as 'Shit FM' and describes our natural tendency to tune into it and then stay there; so if we can't turn it off, how do we escape this damaging monologue? She recommends that we tell our 'Circle of Safety', or our Troop, when we are stuck in that cycle, and literally text a trusted person with 'I am stuck listening to "Shit FM" – do you have time for a chat/coffee?' We need to have an efficient way of telling people that we need help to shift out of our negative thoughts and feelings. I am not saying, and neither does Russell, that we have to be positive all the time, because it is important that we address our negative emotions and sometimes stay with them for a while, but we must be careful that this does not turn into an extended stream of negativity about ourselves. I love the analogy that it is okay to be a hippo at times and wallow in the mud that might be sadness or shame, but there comes a time when you must get yourself out of there and shake all that mud off. Remember, negative thinking creates anxiety and stress, which leads to you becoming both physically and mentally unwell.

How do we start to remove ourselves from this cycle and learn to be more compassionate to ourselves? Russell recommends that for a short period of time, we pay attention to our language and ask ourselves the following questions:

- How do I speak about others?
- How do I speak about myself?
- Is my language empowering or disempowering?
- Do I use self-depreciating language?
- Do I tell stories that make me feel bad about myself?

Whether you are speaking out loud or in your head, try to reframe the negative and harness the power of positivity in your self-talk. Coaches will often tell you to talk to yourself in the second person – 'I am failing' can be reframed to 'You are doing your best.' This type of self-talk can feel uncomfortable and contrived to begin with; I certainly found myself cringing at my first attempts. However, if you persist, it becomes an effective way to recognise your emotions and to rationalise what it is you're attempting to get done. You will often realise that any feeling of failure is only due to setting yourself impossibly high expectations. This goes back to that pillar of self-awareness.

Take a moment:

- **Ask yourself the questions above. Your answers will make interesting reading.**
- **Think about what you could change and do this for a week and see how that feels.**
- **Start to focus on what you know about yourself rather than what you *think* about yourself.**

Compassionate leadership and coaching

The word 'Coach' means different things to people, and it is an industry which is growing exponentially. A quick search on the internet for the word 'coach' gave me the following:

- Executive Coach.
- Career Coach.
- Business Coach.
- Relationship Coach.
- Health Coach.
- Leadership Coach.
- Depression Coach.
- Holistic Coach.
- Transformational Coach.
- Democratic Coach.
- Sales Coach.
- Success Coach.
- Motivational Coach.
- Lifestyle Coach.
- Spiritual Coach.

- Mental Health Coach.
- ADHD Coach.
- Teams Coach.
- Performance Coach.
- Legacy Coach.
- Sexual Coach.

What is coaching?

You can be forgiven for being confused about the role and what coaching can do for you. In the UK, anyone can say that they are a coach, but I would recommend finding someone who is at least qualified as a level 5 or higher, as that shows that they have been trained in what is a quite challenging process. I am qualified to level 5 as a Performance Coach with NLP (neurolinguistic programming), this course took over a year to complete with a very robust assessment process which involved filming coaching sessions and reflecting on my practice. Despite this, I still find it easier to tell clients what coaching *isn't* rather than what it *is*.

Coaching is neither counselling nor mentoring – both have their place in human interactions and can be incredibly powerful, but coaching is different to both. Counselling can be simply defined as talking therapy with a trained professional to work through emotional and psychological issues. Counselling comes in many forms, and I believe that most people would benefit from it at some point in their lives. Alternatively, being a mentor, particularly in teaching, is about taking on the role of the guide or expert and supporting someone with their professional growth. A mentor will often give their mentee advice based on strategies that have worked for them, from experiences that have been part of their own professional development. If a trainee teacher has a good and experienced mentor, it can make all the difference to them as they learn and grow in confidence.

Duncan Partridge in his book *Coaching for Educators. How to Transform CPD in Your School* (2022) defines mentoring as:

> Expert support, often but not solely, provided to professionals who are new in their roles, where the focus is on the offering of advice and sharing of knowledge.

What is mentoring?

As a teacher, I mentored many student teachers, and the majority went on to become excellent practitioners; I got huge personal and professional fulfilment from doing this. At present, I have an associate personal tutor role with Best Practice Network, which involves me supporting trainee teachers in primary schools in the southeast of England. I love this role, because I really enjoy interacting with people at the beginning of their teaching career and it fills me with optimism and pride.

When I trained to be a coach, I initially found it very hard to adjust to the differences between coaching and mentoring, and when I was coached by Dr. Emma Kell, I found the sessions exhausting – it is not for the faint hearted. Why? Well, it was because I believed my coach would tell me how to change things, how to manage my work-life balance and stop feeling like a failure or at least give me suggestions like a mentor would. But no – she asked me more and more questions and made me think harder and harder – she challenged my self-belief, and this took me on a whole different path. Of course, Emma is an incredible coach, and she was playing her role to perfection, but it is challenging on both sides of those conversations. If you are being coached at all, it is for a reason, and as a coach you want to help and support that person, so sometimes it is almost impossible to stop yourself saying, 'If I were you…'. But good coaches do not do that.

What is coaching then? (I hear you ask). There are lots of different methods of coaching and some of them completely contradict each other, so I will tell you what works for me when I coach.

How I coach

Coaching is a series of one-to-one conversations with an individual who has recognised that they want to make changes professionally or personally (I tend to stick with the professional, but the personal will often play a role). It is about setting goals, committing to the process and always being future focused. Sometimes, clients (coachees) cannot identify exactly what it is they want to achieve, and so I would start with, 'What do you no longer want in your life?' Coaching is about reframing problems, changing your perspective and exploring your self-limiting beliefs. Many coaches are trained using the GROW model (Goal, Reality, Will, Options), but there are lots of other effective methods to explore.

Since qualifying, I have coached teachers out of teaching, and I have coached them back to the joy of the job. Whilst coaching teachers *out* of the profession may seem like a terrible idea during a recruitment and retention crisis, I do believe that when someone has nothing left to give in the classroom, coaching is a way of finding them new purpose elsewhere. After all, coaching, as well as ill health, was instrumental in my decision to leave headship, but here I am still passionate about supporting the pupils and adults in our education system, this time coming at it from a different perspective.

Here is a snapshot of the impact coaching can have on us:

Teaching is hard work at the best of times but teaching a particularly challenging class had almost finished me off! I felt broken. I began to question my abilities as a teacher, and my self-esteem was lower than it had ever been.

Unable to find a work life balance, I knew that I was burning out. I decided to give it another year before I considered leaving the profession that I had worked so long and hard to be a part of. My very supportive head teacher suggested I access coaching with Sarah. Here began my healing process. Sarah oozes warmth, compassion, empathy and logic. Her personality and professionalism offered a safe space to talk, rant and reflect upon my immediate thoughts and reactions in difficult situations. I truly believe that my weekly coaching sessions with Sarah have given me strategies and perspective. I have learned to better understand my initial thoughts and reactions, and how they affect others. I am beginning to believe in myself again and when difficult situations arise, I remember to tell myself that 'it's not personal' and that 'I am trying my best.' 'Sarah made me feel valued and seen from the moment I met her. She has clear and strong values which encompassed each of our sessions. Sarah has helped me to believe in myself and believe in the job I do. I have found a love for what I do again - thank you!'

For the past 6 years Sarah has taught, guided and supported me to be the best I can be. She is knowledgeable, kind as well as being extremely caring (and hilarious!) If Sarah hadn't believed in me, and pushed me to progress in my career, I wouldn't be where I am today and for that I am eternally grateful. Thanks to Sarah I now believe in myself and have grown immensely in confidence. I feel extremely lucky for getting to work with Sarah and for all her support and knowledge shared.

The link between coaching and compassionate leadership

Coaching and compassionate leadership are a very powerful combination that can create for your school highly effective professional development across all members of your team. Schools where this works well have used a combination of individual coaching and group coaching to ensure everyone can learn from the process. There is a pertinent and well-used quote from Dylan William, 'Every teacher needs to improve, not because they are not good enough, but because they can be even better'.

The importance of psychological safety

To get coaching right, it needs to be carried out with the right intentions, in the right environment, and should never be used as a tool to judge or as evidence in any form of competency-based systems. This relies on the assumption that you are at least well on the way to creating a culture where people feel safe enough to show some vulnerability and to be trusted to make decisions about their practice. Any kind of work environment must create a feeling of psychological safety for all those who work there – this is crucial for schools, not just for their staff but for the pupils who attend. If you don't have psychological safety in your workplace, then toxicity can take hold, and no one wants to work in a toxic environment apart from those that have created it and perpetuated it.

Psychological safety is a term first used by Carl Rodgers in the 1960s, and he referred to it as creating the conditions, in a home, school or workplace where the members are made to feel that they have unconditional worth. In other words, to know that those around you will hold you in high regard even if you make mistakes, or at times are unable to regulate yourself emotionally.

Take a moment:

- **I wonder how many young people really feel psychologically safe in our classrooms?**
- **How many of our young people feel that their worth is linked to how they behave in school? The same questions can be asked of the staff we lead, and, of course, to ourselves?**
- **How psychologically safe do you feel in your setting?**

Let me give you an example.
Imagine this scenario:

A child who attends your school is often late for school, and for most of the time it is just a few minutes, but it is after the register and so she must come into the school office unaccompanied to sign in. When she arrives in the office, there is always at least one member of staff on the reception desk and other staff doing administrative tasks or collecting resources for their teaching. The receptionist will invariably greet the young person by pointing out she is late, telling her how many minutes of learning she has missed and asking her to sign in. Often the young person does not respond verbally, and this will also be commented by either the receptionist or another member of staff. The young person signs in and goes to her class, where she will often be greeted in the same manner. Attendance is under scrutiny in this school, as in most, and this pupil has been deemed to be vulnerable, due to several recent safeguarding concerns.

Why is this not an appropriate way to deal with this situation – think about psychological safety?

Firstly, what the receptionist knows about this young person is minimal and will be based on her own perceptions and personal biases (she may know of the family!). There are multitude of reasons why the pupil is late for school, but she is unlikely to tell anyone in this situation because she will not be feeling safe or valued enough to do so. Also, there are other members of staff present who should not be privy to this information. If this young person has already had a chaotic start to the day at home, this will only make her feel worse. Hopefully, most of you will be thinking that this would not happen in your school and this makes me happy.

However, in my different roles visiting schools, I spend a lot of time waiting is school reception areas, generally just as the school day begins and believe me, I still see and hear this far too often.

The alternative greeting, of course, would be much more positive – a well done for getting to school perhaps, followed by a member of staff picking her up to discreetly check to see if they had eaten and if they needed some time to regulate before entering the class.

Which one supports an environment of psychological safety and a culture of kindness?

In 1999, Dr. Amy. C. Edmondson began to apply this idea more in the business world, with a view to getting the best results from your staff. The basic claims in her research are that if you create the correct environment, people will be more willing to speak up in meetings, take risks and share their ideas without the risk of being ignored or dismissed. It is easy to see how this would ultimately lead to better decision-making, learning and innovation.

Surely, this is what we want for our schools as well as our industries.

As I mentioned in the earlier pages of this book, one of the most important things to consider whilst leading in a school is that every single one is made up of people, and in a school where you are getting things *right,* the majority of those people are all trying to accomplish the same thing. However, it doesn't necessarily follow that they will all want or need to accomplish that goal in the same way using the same strategies. (This is, of course, why some non-negotiables will never work.) In any group, or troop, or tribe of people where you are trying to create something worthwhile and productive collectively, there are several elements to remember. Each one of those people brings their whole life's worth of experiences, perspectives, biases (conscious and unconscious), strengths and weaknesses with them, and all these resources can be tapped into. If those around you feel that their worth is not conditional, then they will feel comfortable speaking up, contributing to the dialogue and asking questions; this is when you and others can respectfully challenge or disagree with them without it becoming personal. We would all like to think that as professionals we do not go into any work situation with pre-formed opinions or biases about others; however, this is part of our nature as emotional beings.

How does this work in practice?

Personally, and I know that I am alone in this, I have spent many years, respectfully disagreeing with others about the labelling of young children as 'naughty' and writing them off before they were even given a chance. The world is changing in its view of neurodivergence and what it means to be neurodivergent, not just for them but also for their troop, but there is still a long way to go. This bias towards pupils who cannot respond appropriately in a 'normal classroom environment' is prevalent in society and still found in our school system. The same applies to young people who have experienced trauma in any form or who are living with trauma daily. Educating people about this is key, and if you can create an atmosphere of psychological safety, then you will empower your community to be able to learn, without retribution, why their ideas can be perceived as outdated, and they can change their thinking in a comfortable way. There are always ways that you can cultivate a honest and compassionate culture that opens your team up to a better understanding of the pupils in front of them and how to get the best from them. A powerful way is to share your failures with them. I hope that the school of thought that leaders in any capacity must be driven, hard on others and judgmental is dying out, and that we are realising that to be like this is to deny our most important asset, that of being *human*.

We should be using the power of our experiences, positive and negative to inspire others to try and do their best and be better to others.

Storytelling and psychological safety

Storytelling (as previously mentioned) is something all humans can relate to. Stories put theories into context, making them real and relatable. When I tell any part of my life story to people (even the parts that I used to be ashamed of), I do it for a reason; it shows that you have compassion for yourself as well as others, it can highlight how you have used your mistakes as opportunities for growth, and for the most part your candour and integrity will be appreciated. And, of course, the art of telling a good story can also help you celebrate all the successes that came with hard work. The attitudes and behaviours of leaders will always have the biggest impact on psychological safety and should not be underestimated.

The impact of coaching

In schools, there are various ways of using coaching to improve outcomes for students and staff. The kind of leadership coaching I benefited from was based around managing my workload, recognising the things that triggered my stress reactions, dealing with difficult conversations and situations and recognising when *good enough* is a satisfactory final product. It enabled me to address my limiting beliefs (that I am not 'clever' enough to be a head teacher, and so many more), recognise where they originated and reframe them, resulting in a more positive perspective. In some coaching training, particularly with NLP, this system is referred to as 'The Three Rs' – RECOGNISE, REFRAME, RELEASE'.

In brief, this system is used to support changing the negative thoughts we often have about ourselves and the behaviours these create. Firstly, the coach will help the coachee to identify these. For example, a coachee may believe that they are no good at working to deadlines, and they are lazy and not competent to do their job. The harder part then is to allow the coachee to recognise where those beliefs and behaviours have come from – do they relate to incidents at school or something from their childhood? Is it something that has developed in their workplace? Has someone said as much to them, and it has stuck with them? Once they have been at least in part recognised, the next step is to reframe them, and this can be done in a number of ways. One of these ways is to find a positive within the negative; for example, a coachee could be procrastinating about getting important tasks done at work, because ultimately, they fear failing. Their behaviour is protecting them from this fear, trying to keep them safe – this is the reframing part. Once this is done, the coachee and coach can work together to think of healthier and more realistic ways to behave instead. This then means that the old self-beliefs and behaviours can be released as they are no longer needed. This sounds like a simple process, but it takes time and effort to reframe and release to the point of the new techniques being embedded. However, I am sure that you can see how this process can be used with long-held beliefs that are related to emotional and negative experiences in our lives, which still have an impact on us both professionally and personally.

Coaching and Stephen Covey's Circle of Control, Influence and Concern

I believe that when senior leaders in any establishment (education or other) are able to partake in rigorous, yet positive experiences of coaching, they will be able to acknowledge how it could be used effectively across the entire school. Coaching with the wider staff will concentrate on the exact things that I experienced – coaching that concentrates on how you respond to those things that are often not in your control. This is the perfect time to mention Stephen Covey again, and this time his 'Circle of Control, Influence and Concern' (1989) – a tool that is frequently used in management, coaching and even therapy. In our busy roles, it is easy to fall into the trap of thinking that the more we do, the more we will achieve; so we do more and more and more, yet we find that somehow it does not alleviate any of our pressures, and things pile up and become increasingly heavy for us to metaphorically carry around. Using this tool with a team, in an individual coaching session or just on your own, can be an effective way of shifting our focus on the things that we can change and accept those that we cannot. In a team situation where you may all be facing certain challenges, this could be a useful strategy if planned for and used effectively. When applying Covey's method to team coaching, it is important that you firstly use effective communication and explain to staff what you intend to do with it and how it will work, then create a clear agenda for how the session will run. On a printed sheet, the 'circle' has three sections: in the centre is the circle of *control*, around that is the circle of *influence* and the outer circle is the one of *concern*. I am sure many of you will be familiar with it, even if you have not actually used it. Every team member will fill in their sheet prior to the session and bring it with them to the group so that what follows can be a honest discussion about each one from this sharing of thoughts, feelings and concerns. You can create

Figure 5.1 An example of Stephen Covey's Circle of Control, Influence and Concern. From the *7 Habits of Highly Effective People* (1989).

a list of actionable points that will support everyone through the challenges ahead (Figure 5.1).

How can this help?

The key takeaway from any kind of session using this tool is to identify that there are certain things that are not in our control at all, yet they are often a huge factor in the things we worry about – we see them as things we must change to succeed; when in reality, this is not necessarily the case. COVID-19 was a perfect example of this – it was something that affected us all, yet we could not make it go away, and we had to accept it for what it was. The circle of influence is about those elements that we still may not be able to change completely, but that we could either influence or adapt how we work around – home learning, for example. And, of course, the centre circle contains the factors that we *do* have some control over, and this is where we need to focus most of our energy and purpose. This makes it sounds very simplistic, but once you accept that there are some things that we just *cannot* influence or change, then it removes us from a cycle of 'stuckness'; in coaching this is called *reframing* – we are looking at something from a different angle, changing our perspective, which is so important. Anyone who advocates this tool is not suggesting that it allows us just to forget those issues that are concerning us, the ones that keep us awake at night, but instead, regularly allocating time to focus on practical solutions to these concerns in order to move on from them and to avoid accumulated anxiety, which will negatively impact mental health. Organisations like Education Support refer to this as 'dedicated worry time' (see website). This is another exercise that needs you to practice, as when you are really worried about something, it seems impossible to switch those thoughts off, but learning this strategy for managing stress can be productive in both a personal and a professional context.

The two circles exercise from Dr. Emma Kell

Another excellent exercise in the initial stages of one-to-one coaching (that I learnt from Dr. Emma Kell) that can give you the same kind of productive discussion is to ask your coachee to draw two circles on a piece of paper: in one of them note down how they ordinarily feel and in the other how they would *like* to feel; this then gives you the talking point of what needs to happen in order to move from one circle to another. From these discussions, an action plan can be formulated in which achievable goals are created; the pathway that opens makes a clear connection from problem to solution, and something concrete to attach their actions to.

Below is an example from an initial coaching session I had with an assistant head teacher in a large primary school, who was looking at leaving the profession. She did not and is now actively looking for headships (Figure 5.2).

Responsive coaching

Many schools are rolling out a different kind of coaching, which is focused purely on what goes on in the classroom, and if done well will enable teaching and learning to improve – which is a teacher's core purpose. Josh Goodrich's book *Responsive Coaching* (2024) is an excellent guide that models the process for you and describes it as 'evidence-informed instructional coaching that works for every teacher in your school'.

Educator and author, Doug Lemov, says of the book *Responsive Coaching* 'practical, wise and research-informed... For those whose work involves helping teachers to become the best versions of themselves, it will be indispensable'.

A fellow coach and colleague of my own is currently studying this book, and the work of other experts in this field, and intends to start using these techniques

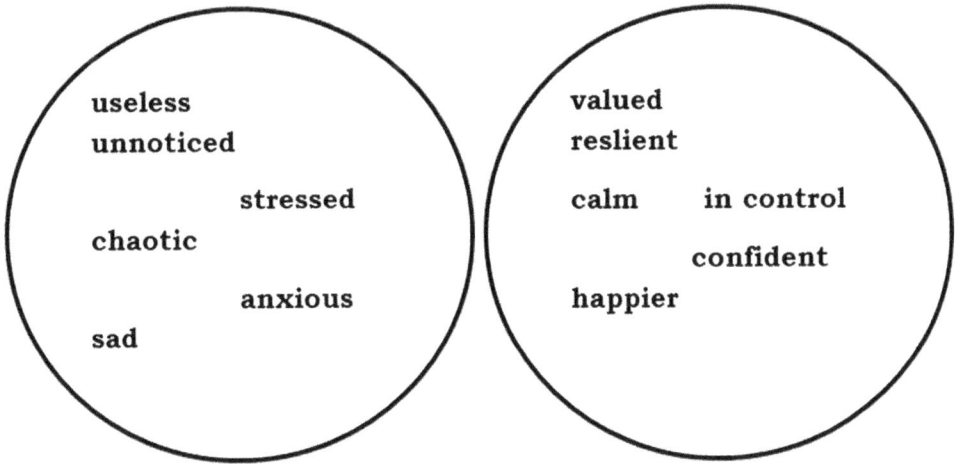

Figure 5.2 An example of the Two Circles Exercise – introduced to me by Dr. Emma Kell during our coaching sessions.

to coach teachers in his local area – I cannot wait to see how it works and what the impact will be. Of course, the idea of coaching teachers to be better at teaching is not a new concept, in the same way that embedding formative assessment by Dylan William and School, Students and Teachers (SSAT) are also not, but we know that evidence-informed programmes work, because we can see the results and measure the success. The way Josh Goodrich's book, and the work of Sarah Cottinghat and others are set out and explained makes the process very clear and easy to apply in your classrooms.

In his book, Josh Goodrich has a section on implementation, which is often the hardest bit of any whole school change, and within this section he talks about the importance of trust – something that I have already talked about in this book. The Education Endowment Foundation (EEF) have produced an excellent report on this subject, which should be a key document for any lasting change in schools: 'A School's Guide to Implementation. Maximise the Impact of New Approaches and Practices' (April 2024).

Having the right culture for coaching

Having got this far in my book (thank you for sticking with me), you will, I think, recognise that introducing coaching in school must rely heavily on the culture being right. If coaching is carried out in a way that is not true to its definition, then it can have a hugely negative impact on the school community – a coach should not be asked to collect evidence about a teacher or feed it back to school leaders so it can be used in any kind of performance assessment and management or capability process. Sadly, I have heard many times of it being used in this way, and it frustrates me, as well as making me disappointed for those involved, because it is the misuse of a valuable resource. If you offer your staff coaching, but then find yourself in a position where you need to start a formal process, then you must still do it (remember courageous conversations), as long as you do not use the actual coaching itself as a catalyst for this or the conduit through which that process moves. Having non-judgemental, supportive coaching systems in place in your school, which are invaluable, can go a very long way to improve or embedding your culture of compassion, which is, of course, based on trust and belonging.

Let me give you an example.
Imagine this scenario:

In a secondary school, an assistant head teacher who has responsibility for 'Teaching and Learning' is also given the role of 'Lead Learning Coach'. They usually lead staff training on pedagogy and effective strategies and are excited about this new element of their role as they recognise that coaching is a highly effective form of professional development. During the summer break, this member of staff spends a significant amount of time researching and planning a coaching model for their setting. After the first six weeks of the new academic year, they are asked to meet with the Head teacher and Deputy Head teacher to discuss how the model works and the initial steps that had been made. During this meeting, it became very clear to the coach that executive leaders wanted them to use coaching as a way to manage performance. They would direct the coach to particular staff members that they perceived to be the weaker ones and asked them to collect information that could be used in conjunction with the school's capability procedures.

Why is this not an effective or appropriate way of using coaching as a professional development tool?

There are many reasons why this is ineffective practice when coaching colleagues. Most significantly, the process should be non-judgemental and goals that are identified are often by the person who is being coached and certainly not by a leader who is not part of the process and has their own preconceptions about the need for improvement. As you read more details below, you will be able to highlight other reasons why this will not work. Imagine the disappointment of the coach who thought they had been tasked to create and embed something really valuable.

To truly establish a culture of coaching in schools and colleges, the following factors are essential:

- Listening to understand.
- Asking powerful questions.
- Challenging and supporting.
- Establishing accountability.

We know that teaching is not an easy thing to do well; the more we learn about how the brain works and what learners need to succeed, the more complicated it becomes. Standing in front of 30 pupils of any age or stage and simply imparting knowledge and facts is not *teaching;* for it to be done well, *learning* actually has to take place – this sounds simple, but most of you know it is not. Coaching in all forms is about changing habits and reframing our limiting beliefs. It is difficult for anyone to achieve these goals without direction, and this is why trust matters so much. To get better at what we do, we need to allow ourselves to be vulnerable, to accept support and to be confident that we will not be penalised for taking those risks. And so, we return to the importance of psychological safety.

According to Megan Tschannen-Moran who has written at least two books about coaching in schools,

> Trust is one's willingness to be vulnerable to another, based on the confidence that the other is benevolent, honest, open, reliable and competent.

To enable your team to embrace coaching as one of the most impactful forms of continuing professional development, they need to be able to open themselves up and put their trust in the coach and the process itself. A coach is not an Ofsted inspector nor are they a school improvement partner, although wouldn't it be wonderful if both accountability roles had an element of coaching in them?

Coaching is an investment in your staff and in yourself. It is not a simple process nor is it a quick fix, yet it results in improvements on all levels and creates a feeling of self-efficacy in your staff, and ultimately in your learners.

Self-efficacy: what is it? Why is it important?

Several years ago, I was introduced to the concept of self-efficacy by someone who was leading school improvement across my local authority. I am not ashamed to admit that until that point, I had not heard the phrase used before; however, I like to think that it is something that I have always promoted. A simple way of explaining self-efficacy is to say that it is a person's belief in their ability to succeed in a particular situation. The theory of self-efficacy was first published in a paper by American psychologist, Albert Bandura in 1977, *Self-Efficacy: Toward a Unifying Theory of Behavioural Change*, and since this time, it has arguably become one of the most studied areas of psychology. According to Bandura, self-efficacy is part of the self-system comprised of a person's attitudes, abilities and cognitive skills, which plays a major role in how we perceive and respond to different situations. Self-efficacy is an essential part of this self-system. When Sam Sillito uses the theory of self-efficacy with her staff, the focus is not just about what her staff believe they can achieve personally, but it also means changing the narrative about what their pupils can do. She will always challenge those who have a negative narrative about the pupils in the school and what they can achieve; this can be a difficult task in a school where opinions about success are negative, and the culture is not compassionate.

Self-efficacy and coaching

If you look at self-efficacy from a coaching perspective, then it is important to give your coachees opportunities to develop this. As leaders, we can influence our own attitudes and behaviours through reflecting on the times that we have succeeded with a goal or overcome a challenge and learned from this. This will develop our own self-efficacy beliefs – in turn, we can ask our staff to mirror these activities with their own successes, and we can do the same with the learners in our classrooms. If we can develop a strong self of self-efficacy in others, they are often able to:

- Become more interested in the activities in which they participate.
- Form a stronger sense of commitment to their interests and activities.
- Recover quickly from setbacks and disappointments.
- View challenging problems as tasks to be mastered.

Self-efficacy and social modelling

Bandura argued that one of the most effective ways of building your self-efficacy is through 'mastery experiences' (Bandura, 1977), and we are now seeing this being translated into the school curriculum. Another way of supporting self-efficacy is through 'social modelling' – this is when we witness other people who we can relate to in some form or other succeed through their own efforts and their beliefs in their own abilities. I very recently shared a photo of my eldest daughter who has just passed her final medical exams and will be starting work as a resident doctor in the summer. This sort of accomplishment is something that university students achieve with dedication and hard work, and we should recognise their achievements, as where would we be without doctors? However, Holly has ADHD and autism, as well as experiencing significant early childhood trauma, and so her achievement is a stunning real-life example of showing others that these factors, despite being difficult, do not have to stop you succeeding. It must have resonated, as the last time I checked on LinkedIn it had been viewed 116,525 times and been reposted literally around the world – nothing else I have posted on this platform has ever had this type of response. The power of social modelling should not be underestimated. According to Bandura, 'Seeing people similar to oneself succeed by sustained effort raises observers' beliefs that they too possess the capabilities to master comparable activities to succeed' (1977).

Take a moment:

- Use Stephen Covey's Circle of Control, Influence and Concern to examine the current challenges in your professional life. What can you reframe, and how does this make you feel?

- Reflect on your own self-efficacy – do you believe that you can achieve the goals you have? Do you look to others as social models? Who are they and why?

Bibliography

Bandura, A. (1977) Self-Efficacy: Toward a Unifying Theory of Behavioural Change. *Psychological Review*, 84(2), 191–215.

Covey, S. (1989) *The 7 Habits of Highly Effective People*. Simon & Schuster.

Goodrich, J. (2024) *Responsive Coaching: Evidence-informed Instructional Coaching That Works for Every Teacher in Your School*. John Catt Educational Ltd.

Ishannen-Moran, M. (2004) *Trust Matters*. Jossy-Bass.

Partridge, D. (2022) *Coaching for Educators: How to Transform CPD in your School*. Open University Press – An Imprint of McGraw-Hill Education.

Russell, H. (2021) *How to be Sad: Everything I Have Learnt about Getting Happier by Being Sad Better*. Harper One.

Sinek, S. (2019) *Leaders Eat Last: Why Some Teams Pull Together and Others Don't*. Penguin Random House.

Possibilities and perspectives: the future of school leadership

This final chapter will explore and recap on these themes:

- Possibilities and perspectives and how to embrace them.
- How to develop our future leaders.
- Managing workload for you and others.
- The power of stories – why they are so important.
- What have we learned about leadership?

The importance of perspective and being able to change it

Whilst researching and writing this book, I carried out a process of digging down to the very core of what makes a good school leader, or indeed a leader, in any context. I have realised that it is almost impossible to break down the role of a head teacher, to comparmentalise each element of it and then to define and add the desirable skills and knowledge to the specification (no wonder the job descriptions are always so long!). Honestly, if you were interviewed for the role and you were told exactly what it would look like in reality, I imagine most people would run for the hills! However, if you practice the art of compassionate leadership, then you can take on the role and succeed at any level, as you will always have your core principles and moral compass to guide you.

As I mentioned previously, in the months before leaving headship, I was having coaching sessions with Dr. Emma Kell. At times I felt like I was drowning in all the responsibility that the role entailed, and I was questioning how much of a difference I was making. The brilliant thing about being coached is that you are metaphorically asked to look in a mirror and accept where you are at this point in your life and then take action to change. One session that has stuck with me (although Emma can't remember saying it to me) was that whilst planning a future away from headship, but still in education Emma said, 'changing your perspective opens up a world of possibilities'. Looking back, I think it resonated because when I was a new and shiny head teacher, I had changed the school's motto to 'A World of Opportunities'. If I meant it for the pupils, then surely, I had to believe that I too could continue to support and challenge the system that I had worked hard in for so long, but also look after myself at the same time. When I started up my business, I named it 'Possibilities and Perspectives' for that reason.

What do we need to do to support aspiring leaders?

I am aware that my attitude towards leadership could be viewed as idealistic and that you need more than a moral compass and an awareness of your values to lead a school effectively. In many ways, that perspective is a sensible one – of course, aspiring leaders need more. My argument is that if you start and end with those factors, then being an inspirational leader is possible.

What else do we need then to be a compassionate and inspirational leader?

What can we provide that will help guide professionals into a role that they can be successful at, and not become a victim of burnout, stress or physical illness due to the all-encompassing nature of it?

There is no doubt that professional development for aspiring leaders can be found in abundance, and what is on offer has drastically improved since I undertook mine. I am lucky enough to support aspiring heads through coaching on a National Professional Qualification of Headship programme, and I am impressed with the course content, in that it does cover the importance of culture and values. But despite this improvement, there are many leaders that still feel underprepared when they take on the role of head teacher.

What is it that might be missing?

In many cases, it is ongoing professional development that is not always in place for school leaders – we train hard to get there and then stop. Often, this is partly because as leaders, we may feel it is more important to develop our teams, and we put ourselves last. We have this (maybe arrogant?) belief that our school cannot function if we are not on site, and that taking time away will cause problems. This will be true in some establishments but won't be if you have spent time developing a positive culture with a team that will step up when you are elsewhere.

School leaders must begin to start putting their development needs as a priority.

What do we know about effective professional development?

The Education Endowment Foundation's guidance on effective professional development states that for teachers it should be:

> Structured and facilitated activity for teachers, intended to increase their teaching ability.

This is then simply translated to 'activities intended to increase *leadership* ability'. Research now shows that the most effective professional development should not be a 'one-off' event, but it needs to be consistent and developed until it becomes embedded in your practice.

When we think about professional development, we often think of conferences or training programmes that work well in many contexts. But one thing that I know about being a leader is that sometimes what you need more than anything is the space and time to talk. The very nature of voicing your concerns out loud with no judgement, and without the noise of the school day, is essential. This can come in two forms: one is coaching and one is supervision, and they are quite different beasts. Despite being the designated safeguarding lead for most of my headship, I never had supervision (apart from the occasional check-in from a governor) regarding the sensitive and often distressing nature of the role. Now I facilitate supervision sessions for a team in an educational setting, and I can see just how powerful and necessary it is. No one should be left to carry around the emotional trauma that you feel when dealing with some of the most vulnerable members of your school community.

Over the last few years, local authorities and multi-academy trusts have started to acknowledge the benefits of performance coaching for their senior leaders, as well as recognising the benefits of instructional and responsive coaching in the classroom. This has not spread far enough yet – on the National Professional Qualification of Headship, candidates get six sessions of coaching as they progress through the course. This really should be mandatory for head teachers for at least the first two years of the post.

It would be incredibly difficult for me to even try to advise you on how to create a coaching model for your school and how to facilitate it, as this would depend on so many factors. What impact are you trying to have? If it is about improving classroom practice, then you would want to allow everyone to be involved at some point, and this would be most likely in the form of instructional or responsive coaching. If you want performance and confidence coaching for middle leaders, then this would be different in some respects and not for all staff. And if it is leadership coaching for you as a head teacher, then that will look entirely different and be much easier to plan and navigate. There are many experts in this field that have produced great blogs and books – Sarah Cottinghat, Josh Goodrich, Dr. Haili Hughes, Adam Kohlbeck and Jim Knight would all be excellent people to start with.

I do believe, however, that if you can get it right, it will be the most effective professional development your staff can engage in.

Some important points to remember are:

- The school leaders must be committed to the process, and not just the idea of it. Time and resources need to be allocated to make it work and not removed when things feel more important.
- It is often more effective to use an external coach or team of coaches or at least use them in the first instance to support you in setting up and implementing the logistics of the programme.
- Sustainability needs to be key – can it keep going even when staff are ill or there is a change in leadership?
- Identify key people to cover lessons and prioritise this as you would Planning, Preparation and Assessment time (PPA).
- If you are using your own staff as coaches, pick them wisely. Ensure they understand the nature of coaching, and ensure they have some training.
- Think carefully about how it will be a non-judgemental process and how this is communicated to staff – should your coach be a member of Senior Leadership Team (SLT)? It is not about someone being better than other teachers; it is about looking at things from a different perspective.

Once you have considered these points, then you will be ready to plan a way forward.

We know that one of the biggest issues with the education system now is that we are unable to retain staff. Remember the frightening figures in Chapter 1. Head teachers are leaving after just a few years in the job, and one of the reasons for this is that they feel unsupported, and they believe the job is unsustainable. Having regular sessions with an effective coach can have a positive impact on this, as the reminders of keeping your perspective, remembering what is important and recognising that some factors are out of your control can stop you spiraling into unhealthy work patterns. If your governors or your trust offers you professional development, I would urge you to find yourself a coach as soon as you can (I am not advocating for this because I am one, but because it was life-changing for me).

Workload

Workload was discussed earlier in the book, but it is important that we recognise that managing our work is key to leading a school effectively. When you audit the workload of your team, you must not forget to also look at your own. Use the idea of perspective and look at your organisational procedures through a new lens; use a business leader's view and try to find ways of making efficiencies – these efficiencies do not need to be in financial terms, but in time and energy.

Take a moment:

- Where are you and your team wasting these important resources?
- Are you able to pinpoint areas where you can make changes?

Communication of planned events

Schools are busy places; this is a fact, so one tip is to be organised in terms of the school diary. In primary schools, it can be such an annoyance for staff and parents if things are not planned and communicated in advance. Think about your energy levels as well as those of your team – staff and governors' meetings, for example, should not happen in the same week as parents' evenings, and parents' evenings should always happen *after* your assessments are done and not before. Do not allow other people to add to the diary, and don't do it yourself without checking with those team members who will be affected. There is nothing worse than being unprepared for something because you were not aware that it was happening, and having someone say to you, 'Well it was in the diary!'. These all sound like obvious undertakings, but I frequently talk to teachers and leaders who consistently struggle to get this right. In the secondary school system, most settings have someone responsible for this, and I admire anyone who can do this kind of organising effectively – you are unsung heroes!

When we realise that the workload of our team is getting too heavy, we need to act, and this ties directly into making your staff feel valued and listening to their concerns. This has to be done in a meaningful way though, and not on a superficial level; a strategy that is often used by leaders is where you pay lip service to the problems and offer a quick fix solution, which solves nothing in the long run – this is ineffective and should be avoided.

Let me give you an example.
Imagine this scenario:

It has been a particularly busy and challenging few weeks for a number of your teachers. Staff illness has had a negative impact on pupil behaviour, and the SLTs have been unable to find cover staff for some teacher's PPA time. There have also been parents' evenings in one of these weeks, as well as the usual day-to-day planning, teaching and assessments that make up a teacher's job. As the head teacher (who has also had a busy few weeks), you sit in your office, and you write an email to your team which thanks them for all their hard work and tells them they all have to be out of the building by 4 pm on Friday to start the weekend.

Why is this not enough?

If we go back to thinking about a culture of compassion and valuing your team, then this is wrong on several levels. Firstly, your staff stay behind after school for a reason, and that is because they feel that they have important work that needs to be done beyond the school home time bell. They know that it is important because you have told them this. If they leave school on Friday at 4 pm (which I am sure they would love to do), where is the time coming from to do these vital tasks? Are they going to lose time with their families over the weekend, or are they going to have to get in to school extra early on Monday morning? Neither of these options is ideal. So, if you are going to enforce this leaving early as a reward, you need to ensure you are giving them the time to do the things they were planning to do; otherwise, it becomes an empty gesture instead of a supportive one. I understand that this is difficult, but you need to try to build flexibility into your team so that there is always someone to cover when things get tough. If you have a member of staff who is really struggling and really needs time to catch up, then model that compassionate side and cover them yourselves for a few hours; this goes a very long way to building that trust and culture of belonging that is so important. Of course, if the work that your staff are catching up on can just be left for another time and another day, you should ask yourself, is it really that important? Equally, if the work still needs to be done, and this is the case *every* week, then you may need to look at working practices and systems and prioritise the things that really matter.

Thinking about your staff

A book that was important to me during my headship and another I recommend you try to read is *Putting Staff First: A Blueprint for Revitalising Our Schools* by John Tomsett and Jonny Uttley (2020). At the very end of the book (p. 161), they set out a 16-step blueprint for schools, to be achieved by 2030. We are five years away from their target date, but I cannot help but feel that we are still some ways away from all 16 becoming a reality. Three of these factors listed really stood out to me:

- A school culture which unashamedly puts staff first.
- The priority will be the staff, so that excellent staff well-being will be a by-product of making staff workload manageable.
- The only time that the staff will hear the word 'Ofsted' will be when the head teacher tells the staff that inspectors are due to arrive the next morning.

Take a moment:

- Imagine what it would be like to either work in or lead a school that had those three things in place. What do you think the impact will be across the school, particularly for the learners?

Communication on all levels

When we consider communication as an integral part of leadership, we need to think about it on different levels. It is not just about *what* we are communicating but also about *how* we are communicating, and how often we are returning to the key messages. Much like retrieval practice in our teaching, we need to repeat and clarify as much as we can. Communicating is as much about listening as it is talking.

Communication, or lack of it, will always be cited as something that has a detrimental impact on the well-being of all stakeholders. Many years ago, when this was brought up with my team, I shared with them one of my all-time favourite comedy sketches. If you are of a certain age (i.e. a child of the seventies), then you will remember the Two Ronnies and their comedic genius, and there is a famous sketch called 'Four Candles' which is a wonderful example what happens when there is a problem with communicating. After we laughed our way through the clip, as a team we then looked at our communication procedures and made some significant improvements that benefited staff, pupils and carers. If you have never seen it, please look it up and I promise you won't be disappointed!

After the COVID-19 pandemic, we found that our communications systems needed to be adjusted again. The wider school community had got comfortable with using emails as a way of 'chatting' with teachers, which was appropriate when there was no face-to-face contact. However, when the world started to return to some kind of normality, we found that a percentage of our wider community continued to email (which is, of course, appropriate at times), but some messages were constant, and many parents wanted an immediate response. Often these messages were sent at all hours of the day and night. For the sake of staff well-being, we created a new policy which gave everyone clear guidelines on how to contact staff, and more importantly, it set out appropriate times of the day to do this. It also made clear that unless it was a serious safeguarding incident, then staff would only reply during certain times of the day. Additionally, we extended this to cover staff emailing each other in the evenings, as whilst I appreciated that people worked different hours, and some staff liked to work in the evenings, we all have a 'schedule send' option. It was astounding the difference this made to well-being, and it also made people consider the impact it was having on their colleagues when they sent them another spelling audit or reading scheme of work at 9 pm.

Communication is about listening too

Naturally, communication is a two-way process, and as said previously, listening is just as important if we, as leaders, want to understand the challenges that our community faces. In *The 7 Habits of Highly Effective People* (1989), Stephen Covey's fifth habit is that of listening and uses the bible phrase of

> Seek first to be understand and then be understood.

Much the same as Manley Hopkinson's advice, 'Shut up and listen!'.

In his book, Covey emphasises the theory that listening requires time and focus – which is why it is always a good idea to ensure you have the time available in the first instance. I think this might be one of the reasons I struggle with the traditional way of running parents' evenings. If you look at it from a communication angle, you have a teacher and one or two parents, with ten minutes or less to discuss a child's progress. The teacher has their agenda and needs to communicate about learning and assessment measures, and the parents have their agenda which is more likely to be about their well-being and friendships. Two different perspectives, in a limited time frame, are both desperate to be heard, but often unable to stop and listen to the other.

In fact, to be a compassionate leader, you need to become a world-class listener; as we all know, listening and hearing are two very different things. Training to become an Neurolinguistic Programming (NLP) coach has honed my skills in listening. If you really pay attention to what someone is trying to tell you, it allows you to be more open to their perspective and be more empathetic towards them. When we are having difficult conversations, it is tempting to be thinking about our response to someone rather than processing the information we are being given. To ensure this is not the case, an effective strategy that you learn as a coach is to repeat back to the other person what they have said, ask questions to clarify any points and show real empathy. This process makes it clear that you have considered what they have said, and if you then take action, this will go a long way to building an effective working relationship with them.

Back to the importance of building relationships

It seems I am at the point in the book where I have naturally almost come full circle while looking at leadership that is kind, courageous and purposeful. Whilst I don't want to keep repeating myself, it is important to remember that for my message to land with you, the reader (or if I am lucky readers!), I should be sure I have communicated effectively. It is worth saying again – **building positive relationships with staff, pupils, carers and the wider community is essential to leading a school that will be successful on all levels.**

When all is said and done, we all need to feel valued; it's what leaders want from their team, it's what that team wants from each other and it's what pupils want from their relationships with all adults in the school. We want others to recognise how hard we are trying and to celebrate (or at least acknowledge) what we have achieved. Alongside this, every member of the community wants to be, and should be, treated with respect. There is no doubt that the quality of relationships, whether positive or negative, is a distinguishing factor in a school's effectiveness. Higher levels of teacher self-efficacy are associated with working in a culture of support, encouragement, collaboration and positive communication – a culture that at the same time recognises that we are not robots, but we are all humans, all flawed individuals with our own stories to tell.

The importance of storytelling

What is it that draws us to other humans? Why do some people inspire us to act? How do leaders manage to influence us to change our thinking or our habits? How do we understand what another person stands for?

In many cases, these questions all have the same answer – the power of storytelling. We connect with people who tell a good story, and who can draw us in and make us a part of what they believe. We don't like being told what we should do, and we get bored by endless amounts of facts and data but capture our emotions with storytelling and we are hooked. Adults are no different from children in this respect. For as long as we have lived on earth, stories have been used to pass on the wisdom of others in the form of parables, fables, songs and poems.

As a leader in any context, your role is to model behaviour in the same way that parents do, and one of the ways that we do this is with storytelling. There is research that evidences the science of storytelling and why it works so well. Through stories we make connections, by using what we know and teaching it to others. Andrew Stanton, a film-maker responsible for films such as *WALL-E* (2008) states in his TED Talk (February 2012) that we want stories to make us care about things, and a good story does this through the values and the morals that it promotes. Every good teacher understands the power of a story, so as leaders we should be using storytelling as much as we can. We can all think of great leaders with their own story to tell – Martin Luther King, Abraham Lincoln perhaps – but the more I research inspirational leaders, the more I get drawn to people like Dolly Parton. Dolly's own success is a tale of poverty, determination (or 'grit' as she calls it) and love. What many people do not know about Dolly is how much charitable work she has done over the years and what she continues to do. Most of her focus has been on education and literacy, supporting young children to read through her 'Imagination Library' scheme, and at the other end of the school spectrum, her 'Dollywood Foundation' to reduce high school dropout rates was created in 1988. These initiatives as well as her scholarships, building new medical centres and funding research into COVID-19, were behind her winning the Carnegie Medal of Philanthropy in 2022. Yet for a large proportion of her life, she has been labelled a 'red-neck barbie!'.

Being brave about your own narrative

At the start of my headship, I was very reticent about sharing my own personal story, as it felt self-indulgent. After all, who would want to listen to anyone talking about themselves? But that is the point – it is part of our human nature to want to understand what has led people to where they are and how that can relate to our own pasts. The fact that I did not do well academically at secondary school, despite showing huge potential while I was young resonates with many. My challenging teenage years, giving up on further education to have a long, toxic and deeply damaging relationship, has helped me so many times to relate to others in the same position. The fact that my own children's formative years were affected by domestic violence and toxic masculinity was something that spurred me on to complete an Open University degree, train to teach and start our lives again. How wonderful it is that I can use my own story as an example of the power of education. People are always surprised to learn that my first job in education was as a midday supervisor, yet I ended up as a leader; that shows anything is possible with determination and a desire to help yourself and others. And now, I can advocate for young and old people who are neurodivergent, as with a daughter with attention-deficit/hyperactivity disorder (ADHD) and autism (diagnosed at 28) and my own diagnosis of ADHD (at the age of 53), I can empathise and understand the challenges that this brings.

For many years, I could not bring myself to publicly tell my story, as there were so many negative emotions attached to it – shame, guilt and regret being central – but the more I have learned about myself, the more I realise that the pride I feel is more important. This has given me the resilience, empathy, self-efficacy and compassion to be a good leader (or at least I hope it has). What I do know is that when someone is in front of you, wanting your help and support or feeling negative emotions towards a situation, remember that they too have a story, and it will have shaped everything about them, so maybe it is time to try to see beyond what is obvious and to connect in an empathetic way.

Whether, like Simon Sinek, you call it your 'WHY', or you prefer to think of it as your 'story', or the people and places that nourish you, they all amount to the same thing – the meaning behind why you do the things that you do. This sense of moral purpose cannot be underestimated in the world of education at any level, but it is an absolute must for any leader. If you have not really given much time and energy to sit and think about this, then it would be a great starting point. If you want to lead a school for a huge salary and long holidays, I can't help but wonder what your values are and how you would build a culture of kindness. Of course, no one in the profession ever cites these reasons; we leave that up to the media and the perception of some members of society.

A sense of humour

Within all the talk about leadership, culture, relationships and communication, there is one thing that I feel is essential and that is a sense of humour. One of the joys of working in a school is that every day something will happen that will make you laugh, something a child says or does, or a conversation with a colleague. Where else can you work where you get an urgent email asking if anyone knows where 'baby Jesus and the manger' have gone? Or in a lesson observed by an inspector, teaching the 'ch' sound a five-year-old shouts out 'cock!' in a confident voice. I could write a book, or even a series of them, on the subject of amusing situations and conversations that I have heard in schools over the last 25 years.

We have all heard the phrase 'laughter is the best medicine', and studies over the years have found that there is truth in this for both our physical and mental health. For a start, laughter is contagious and can help to build rapport and often defuses conflict. Finding humour in a situation can help us maintain a sense of perspective and realisation that some things are out of our control. According to numerous health organisations, laughter has many health benefits: it can boost our immune systems and protect us from stress, as well as relaxing our muscles and protecting our hearts. Laughter swaps cortisol in our bloodstream with chemicals like dopamine, oxytocin and endorphins, which all have a much more positive effect on us, according to the National Institutes of Health and their extensive library of research papers on this subject. It is thought that children will laugh over 100 times a day, but as adults we are nowhere near that figure. Perhaps this is something our pupils can teach us.

Take a moment:

- **When was the last time you really laughed with someone to the point of near hysteria?**
- **Why not make laughing more one of your goals? Or even better, make it your goal to make other people laugh more.**

What have I learnt about leading with compassion? What am I hoping might have resonated with you?

Firstly, congratulations for sticking with me to the end (if you didn't, then I don't hold a grudge – your time is precious) and I hope that you have gleaned one or two nuggets of useful stuff to help you along your leadership journey. Teaching (as Dylan Williams tells us) is a difficult and complex undertaking, and leading teaching in a school community has many added layers to it. To ensure that you can fulfill all your responsibilities, you must put your well-being, and that of your staff, at the centre, and not at the periphery as some form of afterthought or box-ticking exercise. Be courageous enough to put the humans (and chimps) first! When I coach school leaders or teachers who are really under pressure and starting to push into burnout, I share with them something Dr. Emma Kell uses in her keynote speaking and training around well-being. We often use the analogy of juggling balls when we have lots of things to get done, but Emma makes us think harder about what kind of balls we are juggling. We all juggle a mixture of metaphorical 'rubber balls' and 'glass balls' – the rubber ones, if dropped, can bounce back or roll away, but will not be damaged; however, the glass balls if dropped will shatter into a million pieces which cannot be put back together. As humans we need to think about which balls are which. Some of us learn the hard way that our physical health and well-being could be one of those glass balls if we are not careful. We might recognise in hindsight that spending time with our own children could be a glass ball or time with our elderly parents. This is not supposed to be a stark warning but a reminder – think of it as me helping you reframe your thoughts.

Realistically to be a compassionate leader, you have to treat everyone in the way in which you would want to be treated in return. There are times in all our lives when we need more support and times when we can support others around us – the joys of being flawed, but amazing human beings.

In the words of the wonderful Taylor Swift,

> No matter what happens in life, be good to people. Being good to people is a wonderful legacy to leave behind.

And in the words of Sarah Louise Hussey,

> If you are brave enough to change your perspective then you will be open to a whole world of new possibilities.

Take a moment:

- **Take some time to think about what you want your legacy to be – in your both professional and personal life.**
- **Look back at any notes you have made, or parts of the book you have highlighted, and try to make some sense of your key findings about leading with compassion, kindness, courage and a sense of purpose.**

Bibliography

Bethune, A. & Kell, E. (2020) *Teacher Wellbeing and Self Care – A Little Guide for Teachers*. Sage Publications.

Covey, S. (1989) *The 7 Habits of Highly Effective People*. Simon & Schuster.

EEF: *Effective Professional Development Guidance Report* (2021).

Hopkinson, M. (2022) *Compassionate Leadership*. Little Brown.

Sinek, S. (2011) *Start with Why: How Great Leaders Inspire Everyone to Take Action*. Penguin US.

Stanton, A. (2012) TED Talk 'The Clues to a Great Story', available at https://www.ted.com.

Tomsett, S. & Uttley, J. (2020) *Putting Staff First. A Blueprint for Revitalising our Schools'*. John Catt Education Ltd.

Final thoughts

At the beginning of this book, I used a phrase that has developed in our house, and that is, 'Be More Betty', and the Betty to whom I refer is now laying on her bed, snoring loudly as I write this. She is our seven-year-old labrador retriever, who, when I was a serving head teacher, was our therapy dog who came to school with me daily. She is to this day the best decision I ever made for the school community and my own well-being. She chose us at six weeks old, and by 11 weeks old, she was set up in her corner of the school office to fulfil several roles. I believe that during her time in school, she was the ideal role model and regularly showed empathy, compassion and kindness to anyone who needed it without saying any words. She was often the only thing that could dysregulate a heightened child or persuade an anxious one to come into the building. She was able to calm down emotional adults so that they could engage in meaningful discussions with others. How did she have the power to do that? It is simple really: she does not and could not judge those who needed her, and she certainly has no unconscious bias (unless you are a cat perhaps!)

We have a lot to learn from dogs, and this was recognised as far back as around 404 BC when the Cynic Philosopher Diogenes (who is often referred to as the 'Dog Philosopher') declared that people should live more simple and honest lives, akin to dogs. Tales of Diogenes from ancient Greek stories also tell of him, living in an old wine jar and wandering through towns and villages naked – I am certainly not suggesting we be more Diogenes. The great man Plato also wrote in his Republic Book 2 that 'the dog has the soul of a philosopher'.

So, when I say, 'Be More Betty', I don't mean you should sleep all day or go to the toilet in the garden what I mean is:

We should approach everyone we meet with our best intentions, be empathetic to their needs and leave all judgement at the door.

Index

Note: *Italic* page numbers refer to figures.

accountability 9–10
Alda, Alan: *Never Have Your Dog Stuffed: And Other Things I've Learned* 23
Ardern, Jacinda 14, 22
attention-deficit/hyperactivity disorder (ADHD) 8, 28, 39, 41, 65, 89
authentic leaders 16, 24–25

Bandura, Albert 78, 79
behaviour policy 3, 29
belonging: culture of 59–60; sense of 4, 12, 42, 59, 60
Best Practice Network 67–68
Bethune, Adrian 36
Brown, Brene 21–22, 25, 53
burnout 27–28, 63
Burnout: The Secret to Solving the Stress Cycle (Nagoski and Nagoski) 30–31

change 8, 9, 12; in perception of leadership 14–15; using personal experiences 12–13
change curve 56
children 9, 37–38, 43, 52, 71, 90
Chimp Paradox model 42, 43, 45
coaching 67; and compassionate leadership 69; GROW model 68; impact of 72–73; psychological safety 69–71; responsive coaching 75–76, *75*; right culture for 76–78; self-efficacy and 78; and Stephen Covey's Circle of Control 73–74, *74*; storytelling and psychological safety 72
Coaching for Educators. How to Transform CPD in Your School (Partridge) 67
communication 85–86; listening 86–87; of planned events 84–85; policies for 29–30
community: culture of compassion and kindness 52–54; team and school community 22; trust in 54–55
compassionate culture 50, 52, 72
compassionate leadership 59, 80, 81, 91; authenticity 23; in business 21–22; and coaching 66–67; emotional intelligence 17–20; empathy 17; feelings of guilt and shame 7; international school system 15; kindness and 14, 23; negative thoughts and feelings 65; partnership, for school improvement 15; psychological safety 22; rigid and high-pressure inspection 15; self-talk 65–66; single-word judgement 15; 'soft leadership' skills 15–17; tough decisions and drive results 22; transformational change 15
connection 33, 88; human 21, 49
Cottinghat, Sarah 82
courage 1, 20
Covey, Stephen 39, 73
COVID-19 28, 74

culture: of belonging 59–60; of compassion 54, 57–58; of innovative practises and collaboration 60; of kindness 53–54; organisational 35; positive 52

Dalai Lama 13
Department for Education (DFE) 15, 29, 53
Dix, Paul: *When the Adults Change, Everything Changes: Seismic Shifts in School Behaviour* 57

early career teachers (ECTs) 5, 24
educational professionals 36, 38
Education Endowment Foundation (EEF) 76
Education Support 5, 74
Eisenhower, Dwight D. 39
Eisenhower Matrix 39–40
Embedding formative assessment (EFA) 39
emotion/emotional: awareness 18; dealing with challenging situations and 42–44; exhaustion 30; intelligence 17–20; negative 65, 89; trauma 82
empathetic leadership 17
empathy 16, 17, 22, 56, 89
ethos 9, 36, 49–62
Eustress 34

Fisher, John 56

Goleman, Daniel 17–19, 56
Goodrich, Josh 75, 76, 82; *Responsive Coaching* 75
governance, of schools 10–11
GROW model 68

Headrest Annual Head Wellbeing Report 6
Hopkinson, Manley 23, 61
How to Be Sad: Everything I've Learned about Getting Happier, by Being Sad, Better (Russell) 64
Hughes, Haili 82

in-service training (INSET) 21
integrity 60–62

Kell, Emma 36, 38, 50, 68, 75, 80–81, 90
Kelly, Helen 39, 40; *School Leaders Matter: Preventing Burnout, Managing Stress and Improving Well-being* 40
Key Stage 2 (KS2) tests 10
kindness 19, 23, 58; in community 52–54, 59; culture of 53–54, 71; culture of compassion and 52; psychological safety 71; school culture 20; as weakness 14
Knight, James 14
Knight, Jim 82
Kohlbeck, Adam 82

language 23, 29, 43, 58, 65
Leaders Eat Last. Why Some Teams Pull Together and Others Don't (Sinek) 22
leaders/leadership 81; authenticity 16; authentic leaders 16, 24–25; compassionate leadership, *see* compassionate leadership; empathy, compassion and authenticity 16; and life 13; transformation 12; values and compassion 13
Lemov, Doug 75
Logeman, Robert 16

Mayer, John 18
mental health 22, 28, 53, 74
mentoring 67–68
morale 22, 23
moral injury 6, 8–9
moral purpose 1, 89

Nagoski, Amelia 30, 31; *Burnout: The Secret to Solving the Stress Cycle* 30–31
Nagoski, Emily 30, 31; *Burnout: The Secret to Solving the Stress Cycle* 30–31
National Health Service (NHS) 6
National Professional Qualification for Headship (NPQH) 39, 82
negative emotions 65, 89
Never Have Your Dog Stuffed: And Other Things I've Learned (Alda) 23
Noble-Rogers, James 6
non-REM sleep cycles 41

'open door' policy 37–38
organisational culture 35

Partridge, Duncan: *Coaching for Educators. How to Transform CPD in Your School* 67
perfectionism 38
perspectives: maintain sensible perspective 38; future of school leadership 80–91
Peters, Steve 59
Planning, Preparation and Assessment time (PPA) 3, 83
positive school culture 56
primary schools: coaching session 75–76; imaginary illustration (School A, School B) 2–5; trainee teachers in 68
professional development 77–78, 82–83
Psychological Mind 20
psychological safety 70–72; storytelling and 72

rapid eye movement (REM) sleep 41
relationships 87, 89; management of 18, 19
Responsive Coaching (Goodrich) 75
Rodgers, Carl 70
Ross, Elizabeth Kubler 56
Russell, Helen 64, 65; *How to Be Sad: Everything I've Learned about Getting Happier, by Being Sad, Better* 64

School Improvement Partner (SIP) 7
school leadership: development needs 81; time and resources 83
School Leaders Matter: Preventing Burnout, Managing Stress and Improving Well-being (Kelly) 40
schools: culture 20, 36, 56, 85; governance of 10–11; secondary 6, 88; staff 57–58; successful schools 2–5; values 51
Schools, Students and Teachers (SSAT) network 39, 76
self-awareness 18, 66
self-efficacy 56, 78; and coaching 78; and social modelling 79
self-management 18
Senior Leadership Team (SLT) 58, 83
sense of belonging 4, 12, 42, 59, 60

sense of humour 89–90
Sillito, Sam 61, 63
Sinek, Simon 21–22, 59, 60, 64, 89; *Leaders Eat Last. Why Some Teams Pull Together and Others Don't* 22
sleep 41–42
social: awareness 18, 19; media 23, 28; modelling 79
'soft leadership' skills 15–17, 44–46
Special Educational Needs and Disabilities (SEND) 11, 52
specialist support, for students 11
staff meetings 3–4
storytelling 72, 88
stress: case study 30–31; defined 30; eustress 34; impact at work 5–6; strategies 31–34; stress cycle 30–31

teachers: crisis in recruitment 6; knowledge about their students 10; Planning, Preparation and Assessment time 3, 84; perfectionism 38; stress 25
Teacher Well-being and Self Care 36, 38
Teacher Wellbeing Index 5–6, 22, 28, 53, 61
team: common purpose and goal 23–24; and school community 22
time 36–37
Tomsett, John 85
transformation 12, 15, 21
transitional analysis 56
trust: in community 54–55; culture of compassion 54, 57–58; inside school 55–57
Tschannen-Moran, Megan 77

Uttley, Jonny 85

values 49–50, 81; and culture of compassion 52; integrity 60–62; school values 51
Values in Action Inventory (VIA) 53

well-being strategies 31; effective tool 39–40; open door policy 37–38; policies, for communication 29–30; situations and emotions 42–44; sleep 41–42; sleep, work, family and leisure 36–37;

soft skills in hard situations 44–46; and stress 30–36; 'To-Do List' 39–40; in unforeseen situations 46–47; and workload 35–36

When the Adults Change, Everything Changes: Seismic Shifts in School Behaviour (Dix) 57

William, Dylan 69, 76

Winnicott, Donald 8, 38

words 64–66; compassionate leadership and coaching 66–67

workload 35–36, 83–84

World Health Organisation 27

World's Economic Forum List 16

For Product Safety Concerns and Information please contact our EU representative GPSR@taylorandfrancis.com
Taylor & Francis Verlag GmbH, Kaufingerstraße 24, 80331 München, Germany

www.ingramcontent.com/pod-product-compliance
Lightning Source LLC
Chambersburg PA
CBHW062139160426
43191CB00014B/2336